KU-740-804

FRAGMENTS

BINJAMIN WILKOMIRSKI lives in Switzerland
where he is a well-known classical musician.

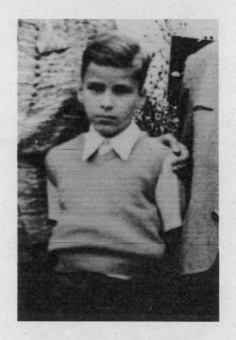

The author at about age 10.

FRAGMENTS

Memories of a Childhood,

1939–1948

Binjamin Wilkomirski

Translated from the German
by Carol Brown Janeway

PICADOR

First published in the USA 1996 by Schocken Books, Inc., New York

First published in Great Britain 1996 by Picador

This edition published 1997 by Picador
an imprint of Macmillan Publishers Limited
25 Eccleston Place, London SW1W 9NF
and Basingstoke

Associated companies throughout the world

ISBN 0 330 34992 9

Copyright © Binjamin Wilkomirski 1995

Translation copyright © Carol Brown Janeway 1996

The right of Binjamin Wilkomirski to be identified as the
author of this work has been asserted by him in accordance
with the Copyright, Designs and Patents Act 1988.

Origianally published in Germany 1995 by
Judischer Verlag im Suhrkamp Verlag, Frankfurt am Main

All rights reserved. No part of this publication may be
reproduced, stored in or introduced into a retrieval system, or
transmitted, in any form, or by any means (electronic, mechanical,
photocopying, recording or otherwise) without the prior written
permission of the publisher. Any person who does any unauthorized
act in relation to this publication may be liable to criminal
prosecution and civil claims for damages.

1 3 5 7 9 8 6 4 2

A CIP catalogue record for this book is available from
the British Library.

Printed and bound in Great Britain by
Mackays of Chatham plc, Chatham, Kent

This book is sold subject to the condition that it shall not,
by way of trade or otherwise, be lent, re-sold, hired out,
or otherwise circulated without the publisher's prior consent
in any form of binding or cover other than that in which
it is published and without a similar condition including this
condition being imposed on the subsequent purchaser.

FRAGMENTS

I

I HAVE NO MOTHER TONGUE, nor a father tongue either. My language has its roots in the Yiddish of my eldest brother, Mordechai, overlaid with the Babel-babble of an assortment of children's barracks in the Nazis' death camps in Poland.

It was a small vocabulary; it reduced itself to the bare essentials required to say and to understand whatever would ensure survival. At some point during this time, speech left me altogether and it was a long time before I found it again. So it was no great loss that I more or less forgot this gibberish which lost its usefulness with the end of the war.

But the languages I learned later on were never mine, at bottom. They were only imitations of other people's speech.

My early childhood memories are planted, first and foremost, in exact snapshots of my photographic memory and in the feelings imprinted in them, and the physical sensations. Then comes memory of being able to hear, and things I heard, then things I thought, and last of all, memory of things I said.

"He who remembers nothing gambles away his future," a wise man once said.

If you don't remember where you came from, you will never really be able to know where you're going.

My earliest memories are a rubble field of isolated images and events. Shards of memory with hard knife-sharp edges, which still cut flesh if touched today. Mostly a chaotic jumble, with very little chronological fit; shards that keep surfacing against the orderly grain of grown-up life and escaping the laws of logic.

If I'm going to write about it, I have to give up on the ordering logic of grown-ups; it would only distort what happened.

I survived; quite a lot of other children did too. The plan was for us to die, not survive. According to the logic of the plan, and the orderly rules they devised to carry it out, we should have been dead.

But we're alive. We're the living contradiction to logic and order.

I'm not a poet or a writer. I can only try to use words to draw as exactly as possible what happened, what I saw;

exactly the way my child's memory has held on to it; with no benefit of perspective or vanishing point.

The first pictures surface one by one, like upbeats, flashes of light, with no discernible connection, but sharp and clear. Just pictures, almost no thoughts attached:

It must have been Riga, in winter. The city moat was frozen over. I'm sitting all bundled up with someone on a sled, and we're running smoothly over the ice as if we're on a street. Other sleds overtake us, and people on skates. Everyone's laughing, looking happy. On both sides tree branches are bright and heavy with snow. They bend over the ice; we travel through and under them like through a silver tunnel. I think I'm floating. I'm happy.

But this picture is quickly scared off by other ones, dark and suffocating, which push into my brain and won't let go. They're like a wall of solid black between me and the sparkling and the sun.

For the first time, the feeling of deathly terror in my chest and throat, the heavy tramp of boots, a fist that yanks me out of my hiding place under the covers at the bottom of the bed and drops me onto the floorboards in the middle of an otherwise unfurnished little room.

At the window, straight as candles and by order of height, four or five boys.

My brothers, maybe.

In a shadowy corner, the outline of a man in hat and coat, his sweet face smiling at me.

Maybe my father.

Uniforms, boots, screaming at him, hitting him, leading him out of the door. A cry of terror echoing down the staircase:

"Watch it: Latvian militia."

Doors slamming.

The man is taken downstairs. I crawl after him, grab on to the banisters, clamber down. They take the man outside, I follow them, and look up in the icy street. Uproar everywhere, lots of people milling around. More uniforms everywhere, angry shouting from all sides. I see a solid wooden barrier, the street is blocked off like a cul-de-sac.

They've put the man against the wall next to the front gate. The uniforms climb noisily onto a transport that's parked on the street. They wave their arms in the air, swing sticks, make faces of terrible rage. And they keep yelling something that sounds like "Killim, killim, killim."

The transport starts to move. It gains speed, heading for us and the wall. The man doesn't move, he's still leaning against the wall right beside me. I'm sitting on the ground, half under the gate, half against the wall, and looking up at him. He looks down at me and smiles.

But suddenly his face clenches, he turns away, he lifts his head high and opens his mouth wide as if he's going to scream out.

From down below, against the bright sky, all I see is the line of his jaw and his hat falling backward off his head.

No sound comes out of his mouth, but a big stream of

something black shoots out of his neck as the transport squashes him with a big crack against the house.

I'm sad and very afraid because he turned away from me, but I feel that he didn't do it because he doesn't love me anymore. His own upset must have been much too much for him, and he only turned away because something unknown was even stronger than he was.

All at once I realize:

From now on I have to manage without you, I'm alone.

It takes a while for me to feel I'm able to look over there, but the man is gone. Nothing there to see anymore but a little mound of clothes, blood, and snow on the side of the road.

I see a tiny room, darkened, the only window hung with bits of cloth. In the middle, a small table, two men and a woman sitting around it. On the table a huge piece of paper that rustles when they put their elbows down with their heads in their hands. A kerosene lamp burns in the middle, lights up the faces. Soft words, almost whispering. Fingers following lines on the paper.

On the floor in the corner of the room, an oval woven basket, filled with rags. I sit on the woman's lap, look over the edge of the table, watch the faces. After a time the woman lifts me down and puts me to bed in the basket.

It's night, terribly cold. A woman is carrying me, there's someone with her, and several boys who know how to walk already. We hurry past walls of houses, we stop and wait several times at crossroads, looking carefully around the corners, then we hurry on again. There's another long wait, I think I see a street sign.

"Now! Move!" I hear suddenly, and we race across a huge, empty square and reach the harbor.

I sit on the dock on a bollard that has a ship tied up to it. We sit in the dark, and we have to wait a long time.

My clothes are all wet through to the skin. I'm horribly cold. At last the time comes, we climb three, four steps up a ladder, and group ourselves in the bow of the boat. Carefully coiled ropes lie there, making a hollow shape in the center. I am set down in this, as if I'm in a pan. The woman sits down on the edge, the boys lie in a circle on the deck.

On my left, there's a tiny bit of light coming up on the horizon, and I can already make out the clear shape of the city spires against the sky as the ship casts off from the bank. We move past the city for a bit, and I guess the way we came and the part of town we escaped from tonight. The woman spreads a cloth over me, and I can't see anything anymore. In spite of being cold and shivering, I fall asleep.

There's a station in my memory. We have to go through a barrier, papers are shown and looked at—maybe false ones.

Sighs of relief and we're standing on the platform and it's sunny. I have the feeling that a danger has passed, but I don't know what danger. People are standing about, waiting, lots of them women, all clean, in pretty clothes, smiling, and with different kinds of funny little hats on their heads, nothing I've ever seen before.

I'm surprised by this peaceful scene. People are strolling up and down, calm and relaxed, and I think:

How is this possible? They don't seem to have any idea what was going on back there.

And something tells me:

This isn't real peace. There's something wrong—it's only *their* peace!

We stand on another track, waiting again. There's no platform, no proper station either, just a little house. We stand next to the rails as if we're in open country. Lots of people are standing with us; we stand and wait, the sun above us is burning hot, I'm thirsty.

At last I see the train, it hisses and smokes, comes slowly to a halt. But it's already full up. People are standing on the steps, hanging there like bundles. There are even uniforms sitting up on the engine, and I'm very surprised that they can sit there in spite of the heat.

It seems to me impossible that we can get into one of the passenger cars. There's a lot of pushing and pulling, and somehow we manage.

A journey begins, and seems never to end. Endless fields, endless woods, and endless terrible thirst. But there seems to be some vague hope as well. I don't know where it comes from, even though the woman explains it to me. But I gather that it has something to do with Lemberg.*

* Lvov.

I don't know what Lemberg is. It's some kind of magic word, that stays hanging and swaying in my head. It seems to be a place, maybe a town, that has something to do with something important we're all expecting, maybe someone we have to find there, or meet, who's going to help.

We never reached Lemberg, and we never found the mysterious person who was supposed to help us. Instead, this was the beginning of years that I only slowly came to understand, when someone tried to talk hope into me again, and took me on another long journey.

2

THE PASSENGER CAR WAS STIFLING HOT, and absolutely full.

"Not long till Basel," said Frau Grosz, who had got me out of an orphanage in Kraków and brought me with her this far.

I looked at her. She was staring at her hands and seemed to be a long way away. Something important, something that couldn't be changed, was going to happen. Basel. The word sounded as if it didn't know whether it was meant to be hopeful or threatening; either way, that's where we were going.

I looked out of the window and thought back to the

house in Kraków, and the other children, the ones I'd watched as they played, the ones I'd fought with.

Frau Grosz might have been one of our children's nurses, or maybe she just came often to visit—I don't remember anymore.

One day she took me aside from the other children when we were playing in the little courtyard. She was rough with the others when they got curious, and shooed them away, and when we were alone, she said:

"I'm going back home, it's a long way away. I come from Switzerland, I came to Poland to get married before the war, my husband is dead, now I'm going home again. Switzerland is a beautiful country."

Her Yiddish had a funny sound; I didn't understand what she was talking about.

"I know they've been very nasty to you, you have to get away from here," she began again, and I wasn't sure what she meant.

Especially because I had never said a word about the children's camp or the children's barracks, never told anyone anything about what happened then. All I'd done was to keep asking about my brothers. That's all I ever said.

"Would you like to come too? I mean, you must say that you're my son, that way I can take you with me," and "Switzerland's a beautiful country."

She was repeating herself.

"People will be nice to you. Do you want to come?" she asked more urgently, because I still wasn't saying anything.

I was getting afraid. Away? From here? Could she be trusted?

"No, no, I don't want to," I started to scream hopelessly as loud as I could. "No, no, I don't want to go away. I belong here. This is where I live!"

I yelled and struggled. But to my complete astonishment, there wasn't a sound. And in the middle of the silence, I heard a voice saying quietly and clearly, "Yes, I'll come too."

This unknown voice! Or was it my voice? I heard myself wondering.

I was horrified. I tried again. I took the deepest breath I could manage. I wanted to scream so loud that everyone would hear!

"No—I belong here! I live here! I don't want to go away!"

And again I heard the unmistakable sound of my own voice, as if it was someone else's, loud and clear:

"Yes, I'm coming too."

That seemed to settle everything. Frau Grosz went away.

I felt as if I'd been defeated, disgraced. I was going to go away, all secretly, just go, leaving the rest of them in this mess.

I could feel the guilt like a lump in my throat. I didn't say a word to anyone. Not even Mila. I liked her. When there was fighting at mealtimes, she always took care of me. Sometimes she even hugged me. She was older than I, and I think I'd known her from before, somewhere.

So here I was in a railway passenger car next to Frau Grosz, who was still staring at her hands and not saying anything.

We'd been traveling for days and days, and this is what I can remember about the last day of the journey:

There was a destination, and it was coming close, it wasn't *my* destination, but I let it happen, I was tired, apathetic maybe, no thought of resisting. I thought about the friends I'd left behind. And often about Mila, who was certainly still running through the streets of Kraków, asking the grown-ups about her mother or her father.

Can anyone tell, just by looking at me, that I'm a traitor, a deserter? My face began to burn, I couldn't hold my head up or look up.

Things started to stir on the train. The journey was almost over. Frau Grosz stood up purposefully, took my hand, and began to pull me through the crush of people from one car to the next and then the next. I just let it happen. I was tired out, despite all the bustle I couldn't keep my eyes open.

I woke up because of loud noises. How long had I been asleep? I looked around. Something must have happened while I was asleep.

This was another car, not where I'd been sitting with Frau Grosz before. And this one was full of children the same age as me, who were pulling down parcels from the racks, all tied up with string, and running up and down excitedly. There were some grown-ups too.

Lots of yelling and calling at one another in a language I didn't know. The voice of a conductor rose above the hubbub, and someone answered: "These children all French" was all I understood, and to my amazement, I noticed that there was a string tied around my neck. Flapping down from this was a label with a red border, just like all the French children had.

How did I get one? I looked around. Frau Grosz was nowhere to be seen.

The train rolled slowly into the dark station hall. Strong arms took hold of me, and set me down on the platform in the row with everyone else, and then we were marched off into a waiting room.

Absolute chaos. Packages were being undone and spread out by ladies, then tied up again. In the middle of everything, children running around and yelling.

People looked at the labels around our necks.

I sat in a corner on a bench, clutching my bundle, though I had no idea what was inside it.

"Those are your things" was all Frau Grosz had said.

Gradually the to-ing and fro-ing settled down. One after another, children were called, then led away out of the waiting room by women in white and red aprons.

I gasped for air—more children were led away by grown-ups—and I couldn't see where they were being taken.

That was the way it had been before, too. Only then it was gray uniforms that took them away with angry gestures. The gray uniforms carried sticks and whips. The ones they took away never came back. But this time the grown-ups were friendly. I tried to push away the tiredness.

Don't go to sleep! Keep watch!

I tried to make sense of what was going on here, but couldn't. The children looked happy, a lot of them were laughing.

Maybe this is all just to confuse me; it's dangerous when grown-ups are friendly to children, I say this to myself.

I struggled to remember, and I thought about the big gray man. The big gray man was a warning to me.

The big gray man guarded us back then, whenever we were allowed out of the barracks into the open air, and we played the games we made up, as we stumbled and hesitated in the bright daylight.

He didn't like us, the big gray man, and sometimes he kicked us or hit us. His gray uniform was all dirty and creased, and his eyes had a dangerous glint in them.

When he was standing there in the middle of us, all bored, I used to think how to cheer him up, so that he wouldn't kick us. He always kicked us when he was bored.

Very carefully at first, then more boldly, I began to dance around him, skipping up to him, then jumping away again, the way you do when you're playing tag. I kept trying and at last he looked at me. His eyes gradually lost the dangerous shadow they had. Astonished, I saw his mouth begin to twitch; only very slowly and just a little at first, but quite definitely. I felt a rush of pride and utter joy. I'd done it! I'd made the angriness go away from his face, and he was joining in my game.

I'd beaten him!

First he grabbed hold of my hand, we danced around in

a circle, and he laughed. It sounded funny and rough, but that was just while he was laughing the angriness out of himself. Then he gave a great swing and lifted me onto his shoulders and I rode him like King David on his snow-white horse. We galloped faster and faster in circles and I was so happy, I couldn't even describe it: he'd been all angry, and now he was playing our games with us.

The others stood around absolutely astonished.

But suddenly he began to run crazily straight ahead, and I got frightened. He broke through the circle of amazed children, running for the wall that marked off our playground, took tighter hold of my feet, lifted me up over his head, and came to a stop for a moment at the wall. He was still holding on to my feet in the air and I flew forward like a loose bundle, clean over his head, until my forehead hit the stone. That's when he let go of me and went away.

He was still laughing.

I lay on the muddy ground, crippled with disbelief and shock at this betrayal. It was some time before I felt the pain. I climbed to my feet and ran screaming at the top of my lungs into the barracks.

A female guard, perhaps a block warden, looked at me, bent over me yelling, and pointed at the freshly mopped, scoured floorboards. Another one stood there beside her, grinning.

I looked behind me.

A trail of blood marked the way I'd come. She threw a big, heavy cloth at me. She ordered me to clean the floor. I bent down and tried to wipe up the blood. Again and again and again. It seemed never-ending. Every time I bent over to wipe, more blood fell down from my forehead, and I wiped and wiped, and I thought:

This is how it's going to be, forever and ever, until everything's dripped out of me, and then I'll be dead.

I don't remember how it actually ended.

So—careful! Friendly grown-ups are the most dangerous, they're best at fooling you, I thought.

I never saw the big gray man in the dirty uniform again.

Maybe he's here, in amongst all these other friendly grown-ups? I'll be ready for him. I'll bite him when he shows up!

I thought about this. I felt afraid, and angry. I squeezed myself deeper into my corner.

The waiting room had gone all quiet meantime, there was only one group of grown-ups talking off in a corner. Bundles of papers were being passed around, then carried out.

The "operation" seemed to be over.

The waiting room was empty.

"Why am I always the one who's left behind?" I wondered.

We'd arrived early in the morning, shortly after dawn. Now the sun was already high, shining through the glass roof. I was still sitting alone in my corner, holding tight to my bundle, looking at the empty room. Frau Grosz was nowhere to be seen. I was freezing cold, even though it was mild. I felt helpless and alone. For the first time in a long time, I began to cry. It felt strangely warm as the tears ran down my face.

I had cried sometimes in the last years, yelled out whatever rage or powerlessness was in my lungs, screamed in physical pain or fear. But when was the last time I'd really cried because I was so sad?

It must have been a long time ago, because nobody was allowed to be sad in the camps. Whoever was sad, even for a minute, was weak. Whoever was weak, died.

But I remembered, and it seemed a long way away and a long time ago. It was in the farmhouse, away somewhere in amongst the Polish forests, where I lived for a little while with my older brothers, long before I was taken to the children's camp. That's where I had my first clear memories from.

I can still see it exactly:

We were all sitting around the table in the main room, and for some reason I was crying. Motti, my eldest brother, stood up and bent over me. His face was full of love and concern, his broad back curved down over me like a great safe shield, and I listened to his comforting voice.

A blissful moment—I had to cry all over again.

But Motti had gone away a long time ago. So had my other brothers. In their place, a strange woman was suddenly bending over me. I looked up.

"I've never seen this uniform before," was my first thought. I felt uneasy.

"So, did they forget you?" she asked, and the way she spoke was strange, I could barely understand her.

I swallowed, couldn't answer, didn't want to, either.

She went away again, shaking her head, with my label in her hand.

"It's blank," she said out loud, turning around.

"Where did you come from? Who gave you this?"

I choked and clenched my teeth. I shook my head, and shrugged.

I won't say anything, ever, to anybody. I have to keep quiet, I mustn't give anything away.

When she came back, she was talking at me fast, and all upset.

I didn't understand a word, but I could tell that she was very cross, that I must have done something wrong, and that the thing "was not so simple," that they "hadn't been expecting" me, that there was "no spot" for me.

But then she went away again, and other people came and asked the same things:

"Where did you come from? Who brought you here? What's your name? We don't know anything about you! You're not on our list. We have to make a phone call."

I stayed brave, and kept my mouth shut.

From the opposite corner of the waiting room there were sounds of agitated conversation. The waiting became a torture; fear and disappointment washed over me, I had to fight for air.

Eventually, a long time later, another lady came in, pushed a stuffed teddy bear into my arms, and said:

"We finally managed to find a place in an orphanage,

but we have to go there by train. Hurry, they're expecting us at lunchtime."

"I want to go to Frau Grosz," I murmured, and started to cry.

She shook her head and looked at me puzzled.

"Who's Frau Grosz?"

Oh—I almost gave myself away.

I shut my mouth tight, I didn't say another word, I just shrugged, and she pulled me off the bench.

This one wasn't wearing any uniform. So I took my bundle and the teddy bear, and we ran to the train.

We were late getting to the orphanage. I was led into a big room, where the last children were just getting up from a huge long table. Someone said I was to wait here. I looked at the table, everyone had gone and I was standing there alone.

The table looked different from what I was used to. It was covered with a big cloth, which hung way down over the edge. The children's plates were still lying there, they'd just left them. But the plates weren't the usual gray tin ones, they were white. Plates like that for children?

I was surprised, and I went closer.

What I saw was so completely amazing that I couldn't understand it, but there was no time to think. I had to do something at once.

The children hadn't eaten everything on their plates! They'd left bits in strips around the edges. These leftovers were all over everywhere, and apparently nobody was guarding them.

I looked around, but there was nobody to be seen. I quickly hid myself under the table behind the protection of the cloth and by reaching out just one arm, began to feel around on top to where the plates were, and I collected the leftover strips. I put as many as I could into my mouth, and as many as I could into my pockets and into my shirt. The strips were chewy, but they tasted delicious; the most delicious things, aside from bread, that I'd ever smelled or eaten. It was like being drunk. I had to get more, everything that I could fit into my shirt.

You could eat enough to be full, and even lay in a supply for another week, maybe longer, I thought.

In just a few seconds, to be able to find enough food to last for days without worry—it was beyond me.

These stupid kids! I thought.

How can anyone be dumb enough to leave food lying around unprotected? They don't seem to have a clue. Maybe they're new here, and they don't know yet that surviving means laying in supplies, finding a good hiding place, defending your food. Never ever leave food unguarded, that's what Jankl always told me.

I was thinking this, and chewing and chewing, and breathing in the wonderful smell when suddenly a hand seized my arm as I groped for another plate.

A hard yank, and I was pulled out from under the table.

I sat there on the floor, mouth full, clutching the last delicious bits in both fists, looking at fat calves and the hem of a white apron. A second yank, and I was hauled up onto my feet. Some of the strips fell out of my shirt.

I raised my head.

I was looking into staring, pale, angry eyes. First they looked at the floor and the strips I'd dropped, then at my fists, then at my mouth crammed full, with the spit running down, and after a moment of silent shock the angry screaming started:

"Cheese rinds! He's eating cheese rinds! Monster!"

I didn't know what a monster was, but I both understood what it must mean—and didn't understand at all. Her mouth twisted with disgust.

Why should it be forbidden to eat what was edible, that nobody was guarding as theirs, and that tasted so good? Maybe the strips belong to her? Does she want to take them back, so she can eat them herself? I wondered.

I pulled free and ran away, determined to defend my booty to the last. So I raced through the room, right around the table, then under it and out the other side, behind a sort of counter, but then, summoned by the screaming, a second pair of fat calves under a white apron came at me.

I fell onto the floor, arms tried to grab hold of me, quick as a flash I tried to bite one of the calves. But all I got was a mouthful of apron. I pulled down on it, got all tangled up, and then there was more screaming and they had hold of me.

I couldn't breathe, so I had to spit out the last of the strips, which produced yet more screaming.

"What's been going on here?" asked a quiet voice from somewhere.

It was the lady who'd brought me.

"He's spitting and biting and fighting, and eating scraps," said one of the white aprons angrily.

She'd already got my shirt open, and now she shook my whole gathered treasure out onto the floor.

Another one came with a pail and dustpan and brush and took everything away.

I didn't understand anything anymore.

They were taking my food away, but not because they wanted it themselves. They didn't seem to be hungry. No, they were just throwing food away right in front of my eyes. Was this how they wanted to punish me?

One of the aprons gave orders, and I was put into a solitary room, as they called it.

"Only till you quiet down," they said, and shut the door.

Only now did I realize that in all the uproar I'd lost my bundle—and the stuffed bear was gone too.

I tiptoed to the door, but it was locked.

I looked around. The only things in the room were a bed, a single one but huge, a table, and a chair. On the bed was a great big cover, all full of air like a cloud. I sniffed. The cloud smelled sweet and clean and tempting.

I didn't dare touch it.

I thought:

The only person who'd be allowed to sleep here must have extra-special privileges, and be very powerful and strong. How else could he defend a place like this? He must be someone with a specially important uniform, one with shiny buttons. I haven't seen any of the black or gray uniforms here, but you can't be sure.

Oh—but what if he finds me here? Will he beat me, because he thinks I'm trying to take over his property and his place? Everyone here seems to be stronger than I am.

Then I thought again about my defeat, about the food I'd lost, and the lost bundle, and the lost stuffed bear, and I was afraid that the uniform might already be standing on the other side of the door.

I listened, but the whole house was quiet.

They're taking everything away from me here.

A lump thickened in my throat.

Perhaps it's not just the food, perhaps they're going to take my clothes too. It's winter. Perhaps they're going to leave me here to starve. Switzerland isn't a beautiful country, the way Frau Grosz said. Frau Grosz lied to me! Frau Grosz has left me all alone. I hate Frau Grosz!

Hungry and exhausted, I crawled under the bed and went to sleep.

3

DID I HAVE FOUR BROTHERS OR FIVE, which seems righter? I can't say for sure anymore. But they're in all my earliest memories, the ones I'm halfway sure about.

Shards of recollection, holding my brothers fast inside, like flakes of feldspar in a great rockslope of childhood memory.

A farmstead, a cluster of small buildings arrayed in a rectangle to make a courtyard in the middle. A house facing an empty stable, a barn for the horsecart minus horse, standing open on the side facing the courtyard, and another barn for grain, now as empty as the stable.

The only grown-up is the farmer's wife, severe, rough, full of punishments. She supervised us, fed us, some kind of porridge out of a big pot.

We sat at a long table in order of our ages. At one end was me, as the youngest, then Daniel; at the other end was Motti or "Mordechaiiii," the way the woman sounded whenever she yelled for him, as the eldest. The others in between, only shadowy pictures of them.

Opposite us, in the middle of the other long side of the table, the farmer's wife, who ordered us never to open the doors or even leave the house without permission, never to look out of a window, and always to duck down when going past one—"because of the bullets that could come through the glass," she said.

The way she looked at us, so dark and angry, as she said this, told us how bad the punishment would be if we disobeyed. But there was also something else in her eye, which made me much more uneasy—I think it was fear. This powerful muscular woman with her big arms and heavy hands, who embodied absolute power over us children—could there be something that was even more powerful than she was? Something even she was afraid of?

How we spent our days in the house, I've almost no idea anymore. I remember Motti's endlessly repeated warnings to crouch before I went past a window, and occasional forays into the open air once evening came.

Once Motti put together a glider out of paper and sticks. I was allowed to watch. He set it out to dry on the little wood stove, warned me not to touch it, and went into the kitchen. But my curiosity was stronger than his warning, and as I touched it, it fell onto the floor and broke.

Motti didn't hit me, he never hit me, he didn't even say anything bad, he just explained calmly what had happened. Then he showed me how you repair an airplane.

When the farmer's wife was away from the house, Motti took over from her as the guardian of us younger ones. This was always a wonderful time. Motti always took special care of me. To me, he wasn't a child anymore. He was strong, the protector who never got angry or yelled. He could comfort too, and he meant warmth and safety.

A canal ran past the farmstead. We had to cross a small footbridge over a weir to get to a meadow where we were sometimes allowed to play. There was only one rail and it was too high for me, and I was afraid of the deep whirlpool under my feet.

But mostly I was afraid of the whale, the one Motti had told us about.

There was this whale that swallowed Jonah when he didn't want to do what God said—or so said Motti. I knew I didn't always do what people said either, and I thought that one day God was going to say to the whale:

See over there, that farm's where Binjamin lives, he's disobedient. Swim up the canal, and next time he's crossing the weir, jump out of the water and swallow him and bring him to me!

Shaking with fear I kept peering down into the water to see if this time the whale was waiting for me.

Motti was the only person I could tell about what I was

afraid of. But Motti laughed and said that wasn't the whole story, and he'd explain why I didn't have to be afraid.

This is what he told me:

"The whale spat Jonah out again, because Jonah said he was sorry. God was very pleased with the whale, because it had done its work so well. And then there came a time when more and more people didn't do what God said. God remembered the whale, and sent him out to swallow all the bad people and only spit out the ones who said they were sorry. But not many people did, and so the whale got bigger and bigger and rounder and fatter. When the whale got old and died, it was huge. And then God had an idea: he saw the poor Jews in the world, and he saw that a lot of them were starving. So he gave them the dead whale, so that once a week for a thousand years they could all eat whale. That's why we Jews always eat gefilte fish on Sabbath."

"But I've never eaten gefilte fish," I said, and Motti said, "Maybe the whale's all eaten up by now—and that's also why there's a war now, because there's been no whale for a long time now to swallow up the bad people" . . .

That's how I lost my fear of the whale in the canal and found out what war was.

But soon various things happened to shatter the peaceful time at the farm. One day we heard a man's voice, loud and deep, half-singing, half-roaring in front of the house. In spite of it being forbidden, we peered furtively out of the window.

Motti said it was a soldier and explained to me what a soldier was. Motti recognized the uniform and explained to me about uniforms. The soldier was carrying a gun, and Motti explained what he used it for.

As the soldier came up to the house, we fled in fear into the kitchen, where the farmer's wife was fussing about. The soldier appeared outside the kitchen window and looked in. He began yelling something again that I didn't understand, and I saw his arm swing back, then hit right in the middle of the windowpane.

The whole window splintered into the kitchen and the soldier climbed in. The woman and the soldier were screaming words at each other in a language I didn't know.

"Out, get out," the woman spat at us, and her voice sounded different, something new about it.

We ran into the living room and listened. We heard terrible noises, crashing and blows, the woman screaming, the man cursing in his deep voice. Then it was silent.

We kept waiting, we didn't dare move, we waited a long time.

Then we heard a soft whimpering coming from the kitchen. Cautiously we slipped into the room. The woman was sitting on the floor in the middle of the room, her clothes all torn and her hair in a mess, and she was crying.

The farmer's wife could cry!

The farmer's wife, this strong woman who could be so bad-tempered and frightening. The stern judge who ruled us children and thought up such painful punishments—she could cry?

I was dumbfounded.

There she was, sitting on the floor surrounded by bits of crockery, between the smashed chairs and the over-turned kitchen table.

"Out, out!" she screamed at us again angrily, but it sounded forced, and she tried to push the hair off her wet face and out of her eyes, but couldn't.

So we left her alone and crept back into the other room. We never said a word about it, not ever, but we knew that the war had sent us its herald.

When winter came, there soon wasn't anything to eat anymore. Every two days or so, Motti led us out of the house once it got dark. Without the woman, we'd cross the frozen canal in the snow and go into the nearby woods. We crawled our way under snow-covered branches, pushed through bushes until we reached a clearing, where a little house stood in a hollow. Other, unknown children would arrive from all directions too, sliding down the snow into the hollow, and going into the house.

There was just one room inside. In the middle on an open fire was a huge pot bubbling with soup. The air was sticky, so full of steam you almost couldn't see a thing. Every child got a bowl, and the soup smelled wonderful.

We went there often, and mostly I came back crying. The way through the snow was almost more than I could manage. Motti always made us go as fast as we could, only he seemed to know why this was.

When we got to the hut, I always burned my fingers on the hot tin dish, and my lips on the hot soup. Most often we had to leave again before I had a chance to drink all of my bowl. But it seemed to be more important to leave really promptly.

Spring came and the ground began to thaw, the weather got warmer, then really hot. We didn't have to freeze anymore.

Then one day it happened. The war reached us.

Sounds of gunfire came echoing out of the wood and we heard the rumble of engines. The noise came closer.

"Under the table! Lie on the floor! Not a sound!" called the woman.

So I lay between Motti and Daniel, my next-eldest brother, I hardly remember the others at all, and we listened to a rattling noise that came closer and closer until it turned into a horrible din. Then there was a dull explosion, and the whole house seemed to shake. The racket died down, there were one or two more scattered shots—then silence. We waited, holding our breath, we waited and waited, but nothing happened, no soldier came into the house, everything stayed quiet, it all seemed to be over.

Having to stay still under the table was slowly getting more and more uncomfortable. Slowly but surely my curiosity was getting the better of my anxiety.

"I have to pee," I whispered and crawled carefully out from under the table.

The toilet was in a little outhouse which you could get to from the main room. I went in, climbed carefully onto the seat, and pulled myself up to the little window. I looked out.

To one side, halfway through the broken rear wall of

the house was some kind of vehicle I'd never seen before. It was huge, looked as if it was made of iron, a gray black monster with a round lid that was standing open. There was smoke and a bad smell coming out of the hole. I could see quite clearly that there was the body of a soldier hanging out into the air from under the lid, and it wasn't moving. Another two soldiers were lying just as still between the fruit trees in the meadow.

A loud noise behind me dragged me away from my observations. The woman had pulled the door open—I'd been gone too long. She cried out when she saw me up there, more furious than I'd ever seen her. She dragged me down from the window and slapped me in a way she'd never done before.

"I'm going to lock you up alone in the cellar for this. No sleeping with your brothers tonight!" she gasped and pulled me onto the floor.

It was already late morning when I woke up on a pile of sacks that smelled of fruit. The tiny cellar was almost dark. The only light came from two tiny windows that opened to the air at ground level. I could see that the sun must already be high. The door to upstairs was locked.

Why doesn't she come and get me—or else Motti—if it's daytime already? I wondered, and listened as hard as I could for footsteps. Everything stayed quiet, there wasn't a sound in the house. I climbed up on a crate and looked out.

It must have been midday by the time I managed, after endless trying, to pull myself all the way up and scramble out into the courtyard.

Everything seemed peaceful and quiet, but there was

nobody to be seen. None of my brothers, and not the woman either. I went through the empty house, all the doors were open and the pot still had some of yesterday's porridge in it.

I went back out into the courtyard, back into the house, back out to the courtyard again; I started calling, but nobody answered.

Where could they have gone? Why didn't they take me with them? I thought.

I felt very sick. I was afraid when my brothers weren't there, and without Motti's protection.

Two, maybe three days went by before I heard any noises. I was standing outside next to the horsecart without the horse.

I detected a roaring sound that was coming closer and closer. A truck drove slowly into the courtyard, followed by a group of strange men on foot. Green uniforms with guns were running alongside them. Green uniforms got out of the cab of the truck, and made a circle around it, and they had weapons too.

On the back of the truck lots of people were standing, all pushed together so that they swayed oddly as they looked down at me. They looked tired and dusty. I stood and stared in amazement, I'd never ever seen so many people before. They were almost all grown-ups, just a few children, bigger than me.

A shape detached itself from the standing group and came over to me slowly. It was a woman. You could see she was different from the others, because she was all dressed in gray. She looked like a soldier on top because she had a peaked cap and a jacket with beautiful shiny uniform buttons. But on her bottom half she wasn't wearing trousers like the ones in green, she was wearing a skirt. And she had boots—I'd never seen any as grand as hers.

The gray uniform was made of some kind of material I didn't know—smooth and clean, no tears, no holes, no stains. She must be someone special.

She stood there, a great gray shadow, and said something to me. I shook my head, because I couldn't understand a single word. She stopped, then she started speaking again, and this time it sounded like the way Motti spoke.

"What are you doing here?" she asked. "Are you alone?"

"Yes," I said, "and I'm looking for my brothers."

Hope was beginning to rise.

Maybe she knew where Motti and Daniel and the others had gone. She just nodded, went into the house, came out again, and said:

"I'll take you to your brothers, come with me," and she took my hand.

I was ready to whoop with joy, but her grip was too hard, somehow, and her hands reminded me of the hands of the farmer's wife.

She pushed me over to the others where they were waiting, the truck started up, and we followed it away across fields and along roads where I'd never been before.

"Where to?" I asked the gray uniform, clutching on to the edge of her skirt to keep pace.

"Majdan Lublin—Majdanek," she said, and "You can play there."

Her voice sounded oddly harsh, and she pushed my hand roughly off her skirt.

"Where to?" I asked again.

"Majdan Lublin—Majdanek," she said again abruptly, and I looked up at her.

"And my brothers?"

"You'll see them all again," she said, looking down at me, and now she was smiling.

She was smiling, but her smile kept turning into a sort of grin, and I wasn't sure what to make of it.

"Majdanek, Majdan Lublin, Majdanek," I said, over and over again. The name was so pretty.

My anticipation of seeing my brothers banished all suspicion.

I pictured how it was going to be in Majdanek, with no angry farmer's wife, just together with my brothers. We would play—that's what the gray uniform lady had said—we'd play, in a big, sunny field outside in the light, with shady trees all round. No more being shut up in that stuffy room, day after day.

Motti must certainly have taken his handmade glider with him, I thought, and maybe the ball too.

I couldn't wait.

How long the journey went on, I've no idea. Suddenly people were saying "We're here"—perhaps that same day, perhaps the next.

I do remember: it was evening already, and the day had been hot. I was terribly thirsty.

We went down a dusty path, past a big snow-white house. I'd never seen such a high house. It wasn't made of wood, it seemed to be made of stone, and I was surprised that I couldn't see a roof. A short distance past the strange house we waited for a long time at a wooden fence with barbed wire on it.

I saw a gate being opened, I saw a wooden tower, I saw a street leading upward, a whole sea of long-shaped houses built of wood.

There were soldiers standing around. One of them was right next to me, and I looked him up and down, curiously.

"What's that funny weapon you've got?" I asked him.

I pointed at a thing that was hanging down from his belt.

Quick as a flash he turned around, just as quickly his arm shot up in the air with the strange thing in his fist, and something whizzed across my face with such burning heat that I thought I'd been cut in two. That's how I learned what a whip is, and I understood:

The gray lady was lying: Majdanek is no playground.

4

THE PEACEFUL CALM of that first sleep in the new children's home was shattered by a nightmare. The nightmare would repeat itself mercilessly in the years that followed, image by image, detail by detail, night by night, like an unstoppable copying machine.

I was in half darkness, and I was the only child on earth. No other human being, no tree, no grass, no water—nothing. Just a great desert of stone and sand.

In the middle of the world, a cone-shaped mountain loomed up against the dark sky. The peak of the mountain was capped with a black, metallic, glinting, ominous helmet.

At the foot of the mountain was a hut with a sort of canopy in front. Under the canopy were a lot of coal cars on rails. Some of the cars were full of dead people; their arms and legs stuck out over the edges. A narrow rail track ran straight up to the peak and in under the helmet, into a gaping jawbone with filthy brown teeth. The cars cycled uphill, disappearing into the jaw under the helmet, then cycled back down again, empty.

All over the plain around the mountain, hordes of biting insects suddenly came crawling out of the ground. Everything was covered with them thicker and thicker, as far as the eye could see, until the plain looked like a sea of evil creatures.

The bugs crawled over me. Ants, lice, beetles; they crawled up my legs, and over my stomach; they flew against my head, and scrabbled in my hair, and ears, eyes, nose, and mouth.

My skin began to itch and burn. I knew I was their last meal on earth. Where could I go to save myself? I saw that the only places they avoided were the iron cars. They slid off them.

But it was no use fleeing to one of the cars. They traveled as unstoppably and regularly as clockwork up the mountain and tipped their contents into the awful gullet under the helmet. Jumping onto one of the cars would only postpone the end.

I awoke with a sense of despair, and the absolute certainty that there was no way out. Any relief is not real, it's the last false hope before the inevitable arrival of death. And I knew it would be both slow and agonizing.

I lay there awake for a while. It was early, everything was quiet in the orphanage, and I had to think about the kennel.

It was during the time when I was living with a horde of other children in the big barracks.

Once, overcome by curiosity, I had gone off a long way from the others; without anyone apparently noticing, I left the inner fence perimeter along with a women's work detail. I went along the road in the camp that led downhill from our zone, which was for women and children, past the next fenced-in zones and toward the big main gate.

In front of the store barracks, where mountains of suitcases and clothes were piled up, I turned off to watch a man in a brownish green uniform. A ragged man next to him was hacking at a strip of earth alongside the path. I wandered slowly past behind them, without noticing that I was losing my direction.

Perhaps they want to plant some flowers, I thought, the way the farmer's wife did when we lived with her.

Behind the freshly dug strip of earth was a fence, and behind that was a row of kennels. I was terrified of the brownish black dogs. But now the kennel doors were open, and the kennels were empty. So I moved closer to the man, to see what he was doing.

Both men turned around and stared at me. The ragged man dropped his pick, and the brownish green man let out a roar of rage and charged at me, cursing and waving his arms like a madman. He pointed to the earth and to my feet. I looked. I was standing right in the middle of the freshly turned strip of earth. Apparently this was a big crime.

I wanted to run away, but the man grabbed at me. He grabbed for my head, his hands reaching for my ears, and lifted me off the ground. A stabbing pain went through my head and neck, and I felt as if my face was being torn in half. But the more I fought, the worse the pain got. I was lifted higher until I swung between the big fists on either side of my face, over the fence in the direction of the kennels. The fists pushed me in, and the entrance was barred with a plank.

Bent over, half standing, half sitting, I waited for the pain to go away. I waited and waited, but nothing else happened. Everything had gone quiet outside, nobody seemed to have heard me crying or calling. A little light came through a crack in the plank, and it was getting weaker, and I knew night was coming.

If only they don't bring the dogs back, I thought, frightened, if only rats don't come once it gets dark.

Rats were what I was most afraid of, because they came when you were asleep. To drive them away, I began to stamp my feet in a steady rhythm, the way Jankl had showed me.

But the rats weren't what was worst that night.

The kennel was full of bugs. The darker it got, the more I began to sweat with fright, the more I tried to brush the creatures off my body, and the more greedily they seemed to start crawling up my legs again. Lice began to run over my face in racing, ticklish streams to my nose, mouth, and eyes. No amount of wiping or scratching helped. They always came back.

But the most disgusting were the hard, fat, triangular beetles that flew buzzing at my head and crawled into my clothes. I tried to protect my hands at least, and pushed them into the semicircular pockets of my child's overalls. But there were beetles in there too, and when they were squashed they gave out a horrible smell.

I was overcome with nausea. My stomach was empty and nothing came up but a sour liquid, and it was even worse than before. The lice were crawling over my face again. They seemed to be in even more of a hurry than before. Neither blowing my nose nor spitting could stop their assault on my face.

At some point the crack in the wood got light again. Somebody took the plank away from the entrance.

I don't know who fetched me out. As I was pulled into the daylight, hot pain shot through my eyes deep into my head. What had happened to my eyes? I could hardly make anything out. The light stabbed like needles, even through my closed eyelids. Guided by the shoves I was given, and blinking down at the ground now and then, I crawled rather than walked until I reached the rescuing darkness of my barracks.

5

THE FIRST DAYS IN THE ORPHANAGE were all confusion. There were so many new rules to learn, and most of them made no sense to me. Everything seemed to happen as endless contradictions.

The nurses were friendly, they didn't yell, they didn't hit us, they helped without being asked, and they brought clothes and food. Especially food!

It took your breath away. Every morning, mountains of unfamiliar luxuries were piled up on a sideboard, and there was enough for everyone—more than we all could eat.

On the other hand, I was always being forbidden to

stick to the most important rules of survival. I had learned that stuff from Jankl in the big barracks, and I took such care not ever to forget any of it.

I knew that everything depended on it. But the nurses and the other children seemed to have forgotten it all. I often got the feeling that they'd never known the rules at all. They did everything with such dangerous carelessness.

Finally, nobody can know how long there'll be enough to eat. It can all come to an end any day. And maybe it's all just a trap, I said to myself.

I knew for sure that I had to be on the alert, because it was the clueless ones who always got into trouble first, and had the worst of it. Each meal could be the last for a long time. But nobody seemed to worry about this.

They always caught me stealing supplies, they always found my hiding places, they always saw through my plans to run away, and took their precautions. But oddly, they didn't punish me, at least not right away. And that was what was so unsettling. What were they planning?

Perhaps, I thought, they were holding off punishing me until they could catch me in a moment when I wasn't paying attention, and that would make it even worse.

I lived in a state of anxiety and watchfulness, all mixed up with breathless enjoyment of this temporary abundance.

But one thing in particular hurt me—I wasn't able to make any friends. I had always been friends with the ones like Jankl, who shared food with me.

Jankl used to steal food, when we were about to collapse from hunger. Jankl knew he'd be killed if he got caught. Jankl didn't eat what he'd stolen all himself, he gave me some, he always shared. Jankl was my friend.

But here, nobody wanted to share.

Once one of the older girls sat next to me at breakfast. She had the most beautiful eyes, and a soft voice. I held out half of my thick-buttered bread, but she just laughed at me and took her own piece of bread from the huge mound on the table.

As for the mound of bread on the table: an almost indescribable feeling went through me when I saw it that first morning after I arrived at the orphanage.

I was the last to arrive in the dining hall, because I didn't know that there would be food for us every morning. Only a few children were still sitting around the table.

I was shown where to sit. I sat down and waited. When no further signal came, I slowly looked up and glanced around cautiously—and there it was! Right in front of me on the table.

A big platter holding a mountain of bread. Clean-cut, even slices all beautifully stacked up in towers and turrets, and behind the towers, more, more than I could even count. I stared in awe, as if it were a holy relic.

Who could it belong to? I thought to myself. Who could be that powerful, and control so much bread? And why was it lying here unguarded? And would this person, whoever he was, give me a piece? Or should I try to steal one?

I looked at the bread and dilated my nostrils. A

wonderful smell was coming in my direction, and suddenly I recognized this smell from before. But this time it was much stronger, and it enveloped me.

I remembered. It all came back in pictures which took me back to the day when I learned what the smell of bread was.

It was a day when the door to the barracks was opened. Bright light flowed in. My eyes still hurt.

"Binjamin! Is there a Binjamin here? Come out! Quick!" came a rough woman's voice from out of the light.

Hesitantly I stood up and went over, blinking, to the silhouette that stood in the open door. The dark outline told me that this was the same gray uniform that had brought me here from the farm. The same high boots, the same thick stockings, the same skirt hem that I had run alongside for so long.

"You're . . . ?" I nodded.

"Today you can see your mother, but—only dahle."

I didn't understand what she was saying. What did "dahle" mean? I still have no idea today. She pronounced it with a very long, broad *aah*. And what did "mother" mean?

I couldn't remember.

I had certainly heard other children using the word "mother" from time to time. I'd heard some of them crying, and calling out for mama. And they fought about it.

Some of them said "everyone has a mother."

The others objected to this, and insisted that there

were no mothers anymore, that it had only been that way once, back then, a long time ago, in another world, before all the children had been brought together behind the fences and in the barracks. But since then there hadn't been any mothers, and the other world had disappeared long ago, forever. They said:

"There's no more world outside the fence!"

And I believed it.

They screamed at each other and called each other liars. They began to strike out at each other bitterly.

All I understood was that a mother, whether you had one or not, must be something immensely important, something that was worth fighting for, the way you fought over food.

"Do you understand? You're going to see your mother! Do you understand?" the uniform lady said again.

I began to be afraid of her impatience. I shook my head and shrugged.

"You're going to come with me, and from now on you're not to talk. It is absolutely forbidden to say a single word, not now, not when you see your mother, not afterward either. You won't ever talk about it to anyone ever, do you understand? Anyone, do you understand, do you?"

The last words came out almost in a shout. I shook my head and shrugged again.

Then she took hold of my chin and pulled it up to make me look at her. All I could see was a shape and a blur that must be the peaked cap on her head. She bent down, stared into my eyes for a moment, and said in a clenched, soft voice:

"And if I so much as see you open your mouth, then I'll . . ."

And she made a terrible gesture over my head.

Now I nodded, and I knew she would kill me.

She took hold of my arm and dragged me off with her. I really didn't want to go. My knees were hurting, my eyes even more. I opened them briefly now and again, but the dazzling light burned and stabbed, and I could only see the path through a watery haze.

We walked and walked forever, big gates in the fence were opened, then closed behind us again. At every gate she said something very quietly to the guards.

The brilliant reflection of the sun off the yellowish white sandy path burned in my eyes, and I was thirsty. My tongue felt like a lump, and my mouth was glued shut.

After a long time of miserable hurrying, stumbling, falling down, and hurrying on again, the woman suddenly stood still. I opened my eyes, she put her finger to her lips and looked at me severely. I nodded again. We were standing in front of a huge, dark barracks door. The sandy area in front of it glittered white in an ominous way.

Slowly and quietly she opened the door.

"All the way at the back, against the wall, on this side," she said, pointing to the left.

She shut the door behind me quickly, without making a sound.

The dim light in the barracks felt good. I could make out a long central walkway, but there were no high wooden bunks down the two long sides: the walls were bare.

At first I thought the room was empty. But then I saw that there were people lying on the floor on covers over a bit of straw, on both sides of the walkway.

They seemed to be all women. They were hardly moving, and when they did, it was very, very slowly. I went carefully down between the bodies toward the wall.

At the foot of the last sleeping place, I came to a stop. I turned slowly toward the side that the uniform had pointed to.

I made out the shape of a body under a gray cover. The cover moved. A woman's head became visible, then two arms laying themselves slowly on top of the cover.

I bit my lips so as not to cry out. I looked unblinking into a face that looked back at me with huge eyes.

Was this my mother, my dahle?

One of the children had once said that if you have a mother, she belongs just to you! So this woman belonged to me, just me? I wondered.

But I wasn't allowed to ask. I wanted to tell her that I wasn't allowed to speak, that they'd kill me if I said anything to her—but I couldn't do that.

So I stood there in silence, clenching my teeth together, and didn't dare move. I didn't look away from her once. For just a moment the face seemed to smile, but I couldn't be sure.

I don't know how long I stood there like that. A loud creak broke the silence, the door opened a crack—the sign that time was up. At that moment, the woman moved one of her arms, groping with her hand under the straw and the lumps between her and the wall, as if she was looking for something. The hand re-emerged, clutching something. She motioned for me to come closer.

I kept standing there without moving. I was waiting, I was afraid. She beckoned faster, more urgently. Slowly I fought down my shyness. I went up to her.

Now I could see the face more clearly, it was shiny and wet, and I saw that it was crying. Without saying a word she reached out her hand to me and indicated that I should take what she had brought out from under the straw. For a single moment I touched her hand—it felt hot and damp.

I took the object, clutched it tight against me, and went toward the door, which now stood wide open, silhouetting the dark waiting shape of the gray uniform skirt and the peaked cap.

We went back the way we'd come. The woman held my arm, dragging me along behind her. I used my free hand to grope the unknown object with curiosity. It had jagged edges and corners, and felt coarse and hard.

"What is this?" I asked the gray uniform as we reached my barracks.

"That's bread," she said, and "You have to soften it in water, then you can eat it." Then she went away.

I spent a long time chewing on the softened bread and then dunking it again into the little ration of water in my mug, and chewing again, over and over again, until the water was all used up and the crust had shrunk to a tiny little ball.

Finally all that remained was the indescribably delicious smell of bread on my fingers as I held them to my
nose again and again.

I only ever saw the lady in the gray uniform once
again. I recognized her by the rhythm of her stride. She
was hurrying somewhere and I ran up to her. I thought
she would look for me and take me to my mother. She
stood still for just a moment and looked at me. It took
her a second to recognize me.

"Oh, it's you . . . you can't see your mother again
. . . it's not possible anymore."

She hurried off without a further thought.

I observed the other children. They were taking some
kind of thick red stuff out of a jar and putting it on their
bread before they ate it.

I didn't dare take a slice from the bread pile in front of
everyone. So I picked up my spoon and went over to the
jar with the red stuff. I dipped the spoon in and licked
it off.

It tasted so sweet! I tried it again. But a smack on my
hand stopped me. A white apron bent over me.

"You're not allowed to do that. Only with bread!" she
said severely.

"But the bread doesn't belong to me," I said. My eyes
began to smart, I felt tears coming and I was ashamed.

"Here's a piece of bread for you and now you can . . ."
was all she had time to say.

"I only take bread from my mother," I screamed at her
in tears of fury, and ran from the room.

But where to? I didn't know the building. The nurse followed me and took me by the shoulders. I wondered whether to bite her or not, but the situation seemed hopeless, so I clutched one arm over my stomach to protect it and held the other over my head and waited for the blows, but nothing happened. I took a quick look up at her—and saw that she was smiling.

So I let myself be led back to the table, but I didn't drop my guard. She took another piece of bread from the mound and used a knife to smear it with a thick layer of the good sweet stuff.

"This is my present to you," she said.

I was hungry, and hesitantly I began to eat.

6

I HAD GOT USED to the ringing of the bell, which summoned us to our walk after breakfast. Like the other children, I'd been given real winter shoes, beautiful new ones of real leather, with soles so thick they'd never get holes.

Everything turned into bustle and hurry when the bell rang the second time. The children got ready to set off.

I was one of the last to leave the table, and I rushed to the row of cubbyholes where each of us had a place to keep his own shoes and socks. It was almost empty—already.

I reached into my place and got a fright: there was nothing in there, no shoes, only socks.

"My shoes, where are my shoes, someone's stolen my shoes," I cried.

I should have guarded them more carefully.

Panic set in.

I hunted through every compartment, but my shoes had definitely gone. The last children had all collected theirs and I could hear voices from the courtyard where everyone was waiting. My heart was pounding as if it would burst.

It's happened again! No—not again. I can't have to run through the snow without shoes again, I thought in despair.

Once before, in the barracks, my shoes had disappeared, and I had to go out into the snow with rags on my feet. Rags that Jankl tied on for me. I remembered only too well.

We were driven out of the barracks in tremendous haste, and then we had to run along a narrow path in the snow, keeping in a column, I no longer remember where to or why. But staying in step was the most important thing.

Whoever had shoes managed better. If you fell behind, you were driven on with blows; if you didn't catch up, you . . .

I ran and ran, but I fell further and further behind, I couldn't catch my breath anymore, I was afraid I'd choke. The children behind me saw that the gap in the column was getting wider, and began screaming at me in fear and anger, to drive me on.

But I had no shoes and the rags on my feet gave me no sure footing. One of them came undone and then it happened. I stumbled, slid out of line, and landed to one side of the path.

It was a raised path. I rolled some way down the bank, sinking further and further in soft snow. I struggled convulsively to pull myself back up, but I couldn't.

The column came to a halt.

The sound of deep men's voices yelling cut into the shrill yelping of my friends. Then I heard a noise.

I raised my head to find myself looking straight at the tip of a black boot that was aimed at my face. I was quick enough to turn away, so it only hit the back of my head. The blow lifted me and threw me clean back onto the path.

Two of the older children who'd been running ahead of me came back, took hold of my arms, and hauled me along behind them, pursued by brownish green uniforms.

My shoes, my shoes, I kept thinking despairingly. The children were racketing around outside.

I reached for the back of my head, where I could feel the big ridge that had formed as a result of the blow.

I thought feverishly.

I have to find rags. Rags for my feet. Rags in snow are still better than socks would be!

I ran to the scullery.

Here there were cleaning cloths. Lots of them, without holes, big, thick, warm ones. I took the first best ones I could find and wrapped them around my feet and calves the way Jankl had taught me in the big barracks. A quick search and I found string to hold everything together. I gasped with relief. I ran downstairs as fast as I could.

"There he is! He's coming!" called one of the waiting children.

I stepped outside. The confusion of voices suddenly broke off. An unearthly silence suddenly met me. A wordless semicircle formed as they all gaped at me open-mouthed.

I stood there petrified, not understanding. Something here was wrong. But now, as if on command, there was a roar of mocking laughter, poisonous and ugly. The children were pointing at me. They yelled and catcalled and clutched their stomachs. I stood there speechless, still not understanding.

What had happened? Why were these children suddenly pushing me away and making such a fool of me?

I began to feel afraid of the unruly mob. I bit down hard and ran back into the house. I reached my bed all out of breath, crawled under the covers, and listened anxiously to see if they were following me.

It was some time before I heard a single set of footsteps, but they sounded calm, not as if they were in pursuit. I looked out. One of the older nurses—she had white hair—came in smiling, lifted the cover, and said calmly:

"It's nothing . . . nothing. Just your feet—people aren't used to that here."

She seemed to understand. Finally someone who understood! She took my hand and led me into the laundry drying room.

"Look," she said, "here are your shoes. Why didn't you ask? They were so wet from yesterday's walk that I put them in here to dry."

7

ONE DAY TWO NEW BOYS were brought to the orphanage. They sat opposite me at breakfast and I watched them curiously and tried to eavesdrop on what they were saying to each other.

They were speaking in a mixture of Yiddish and Polish. I was so frightened that I got goose pimples and began to sweat. My stomach clenched with fear. I stared at them.

Haven't I seen them somewhere before, in the chaotic throng of children in the half-light of the big barracks?

"No," I decided, yet I wasn't absolutely sure.

My neighbor at table nudged me and asked something. I bit my lips and didn't reply.

Do not say a word right now. They mustn't hear my voice. They could recognize me by my voice. And if they recognize me and tell everyone where I came from, then it's all over. Either they'll kill me themselves, out of revenge, or they'll betray me to one of the gray uniform women in Poland, and they'll come and get me and throw me into the furnace.

My head was hammering.

I tried to think clearly, but the anxiety kept rising in me.

Without eating my breakfast or saying a word to the child next to me, I ran back into the empty dormitory, jumped onto my bed, and bit down on the pillow so as not to cry out. Panic.

I couldn't stop the vivid memories of the new boy in the big barracks. They forced me to lie still and for the thousandth time I had to be a spectator at what had happened to the new boy in front of the barracks, and how it was my fault and my crime.

At the beginning there was no one in the big barracks who took charge of organizing things or keeping anything clean. We were alone most of the time—a hundred, a hundred and fifty, maybe two hundred children. At that time there was no roll call.

Most of the children were older than I. When we weren't allowed for long periods to go outdoors, we had no choice but to relieve ourselves in the long passageway between the two-tiered racks of bunks. Nobody cared, nobody cleaned up, until the shit was ankle deep.

Hunger was a torment, but thirst was worse. Even the stone washtubs remained empty for a long time. Then once a day a few women in torn clothes and rags started coming to our door from the neighboring barracks and they brought us water in buckets, although it was forbidden. So we were able to fill our mugs at least once a day, but sometimes there was only enough for half.

But the worst thing during that time was the stink. I often thought I was going to suffocate in it.

Once I had to get down from my bunk, and sank up to my calves in shit. I was disgusted, I gasped and retched, but mostly I cried.

"What are you bawling about? Stop that noise," one of the older boys snapped at me.

He seemed to know everything already and to have been here for some time.

It was Jankl.

I think that was the first time I saw him. He was something like a leader, or a ringleader, and you could ask him things, and he helped, and he taught us lots of tricks. He became my friend, my counselor, and my protector. He knew how to steal food and where to get it, and he shared with me.

Jankl looked at me.

"If you stand in it, it's warmer. It'll stop your feet from freezing so quickly."

I was amazed at his wisdom, fell silent, and fought down my need to be sick.

Then at some point after that, we were all driven outdoors one day. It wasn't so cold anymore. The ground was thawing and getting soft. The big barracks was scrubbed out with buckets of water by faceless ragged gray figures who hurried in with full buckets and out again with empty ones in an unending chain. All I can remember is their strange shapes.

It was almost evening when the endless hurrying came to a stop. The big barracks was clean.

But our good fortune was short-lived. New barracks regulations were introduced; new rules of the game, and you only survived if you learned them right away.

By day, you had to go outside to relieve yourself, but only if you could run far enough to reach the latrine ditch near the big fence. We soon found out what could happen to anyone who didn't reach the ditch in time.

The image of the two boys in front of the barracks door is burned into my mind.

They were forbidden to come back into the barracks. They were meant to be a warning to the rest of us. Huddled over, crying constantly, they knelt in the filth. I stared horrified at their trousers, which were all spotted with red.

The older children explained:

On the way to the latrines they hadn't been able to hold their water anymore. Two of the block wardens had caught them as they were peeing against the wall behind one of the barracks. As a punishment, they'd taken little sticks and pushed them up into the boys' penises as far as they'd go. Then the block wardens had hit their penises, making the sticks break off. The wardens had laughed a lot and had a good time.

"Now all they'll do is pee blood," said one of them.

When evening came they were still whimpering. Then people came and took them away.

But at night, nobody was allowed to go to the latrines.

So nights became much scarier even than the days. Regulations provided for a single metal bucket to be put out in the passageway down the big barracks each evening. But it was far too small for all of us. It soon filled up.

A big block warden watched over the bucket. Her uniform was like the uniform that had brought me here from the farm and the one that had brought me to my mother, only much dirtier and without any shiny buttons. She too always had a peaked cap on her head, and we knew that when she pulled the cap forward was when she was most dangerous.

If a child got up in the night and went to the bucket, her torch switched itself on.

Woe betide the one who first made the bucket overflow in the dark, or knocked it over. He would be grabbed, dragged down the passageway while being yelled at, and taken outside. No one this happened to ever came back. But the uniform left us on our own for the rest of the night. We all knew at those times that we couldn't go anymore, and everything had to stay absolutely quiet.

Those silences were unearthly, and it was a great torture, because lots of us had diarrhea.

The new boy they brought during the day was pale, small, and very shy, and didn't know how anything worked.

He was given a bunk on the other side of the passage-way, diagonally opposite me. At that time we were sleeping four or five to a bunk section on torn sacks oozing straw and insects. We had one cover, and everyone tried to pull as much of it over himself as possible.

It was only his first night and the new boy began to moan, softly at first, then louder and louder, and sometimes cried out. He wanted to go to the bucket, but the bucket had already been taken away, and he had taken in the strict instructions. He complained louder and louder about the pains in his stomach.

"What shall I do? I need the bucket, I can't hold on any longer," he kept saying, and "I can't anymore! Help me, help!"

But nobody answered. There was nothing anyone could say.

We crawled as far under our covers as we could and tried not to make a sound. We were trembling, and the anxiety was terrible. The new boy could be the end of us all with his screaming.

If the guards hear the noise, we're done for, and the death carts will pick us up in the morning, I thought.

Now he was calling out again, and I put my hands over my ears. It didn't do any good. I thought my heart was going to jump right out of my body.

"Help me! What should I do?" the new boy screamed, louder than ever.

Then he was quiet for a moment.

But the sudden quiet was as frightening as his noise had been—I listened hard, and thought I could hear footsteps coming closer to the barracks. Panic took hold of me.

Still nobody answered the new boy.

"Just go in the straw, right where you are," a loud voice said suddenly.

At first I was stunned, then I shook—that sounded like my voice. It *was*.

With horror I realized that I'd said right out loud, really loud, what I only thought I was thinking.

Everyone listened tensely. The footsteps went away again. The new boy whimpered quietly, but it didn't sound like pain anymore, it sounded like relief and exhaustion, and soon we were all asleep.

It was early morning, at first light. We were already standing in a long double row outside on the swampy assembly ground, being counted perhaps. We were standing, and not allowed to move. It went on for an eternity. Apparently the barracks was being inspected.

We looked at each other.

Way out in front, right opposite, but hard to make out, was the shape of a block warden or a gray SS assistant, and next to it, big, threatening, booted, a black uniform.

The sun slowly rose behind the roofs of the blocks at the other end of the assembly ground. It shone directly into our faces. Our eyes hurt; we weren't used to the bright light. But nobody dared to turn away.

Behind us there was a creaking and groaning.

Don't turn around, I thought, they're bringing the cart that collects the corpses.

It came every morning.

More waiting.

Then, suddenly, quick footsteps approaching from our barracks. They went up to the black uniform.

A second's expectant hush, then a terrible roaring:

"Who soiled the straw last night? Whatever swine is responsible, identify yourself."

Silence.

I began to sweat. The whole world was waiting. My chest started to hurt. I was so terrified, I could hardly breathe. I guessed what was coming next.

I tried to think.

Should I identify myself? Protect the new boy? Should I say it? Yes, I should say I was the cause of it.

I stood frozen, didn't say a word, didn't step forward, and knew in despair that my fear and cowardice were winning out.

"Who?" the voice roared again out of the light. "Who was the swine?"

Slowly a small figure detached itself from our row—it was the new boy.

Head down, huddled over, arms waving loosely, he shuffled over to the gray and the black uniforms.

It seemed an endlessly long distance, and it seemed to take forever.

At last he stood there in front of them. I could hardly even see him anymore. The sun was higher and my eyes hurt.

The new boy was now just a shadow that melted into the dark outlines of the two uniforms.

Should I identify myself now? I can still do it. It's not

too late yet! I could say I caused it, that it wasn't the new boy's fault.

I shook. I knew this was the absolute last moment to save the new boy.

What should I do, what should I do?

The moment passed. I gasped for air.

A new fear took hold of me.

The new boy can still betray me. He can say, "He's the one who told me to do it." How long will he hold out before he talks?

Fear and guilt choked off my breath. I couldn't stand it anymore. I wanted to sink into the muddy ground, become invisible. I tried to scuffle backward out of the row, barefoot, and deeper into the mud.

I wanted to sink into the mud forever!

But it didn't work.

"Halt," someone yelled behind me.

And I was back in the row again.

It was one of the brownish green ones, a Ukrainian perhaps, an assistant of the black uniform. They often arrived together. The Ukrainian stepped forward. He inspected us angrily, walking down the row.

I listened up ahead, but I couldn't hear anything. I looked anxiously. I trembled. All I could see was shadows. They were standing right in the sun, which was now fully risen, and my eyes burned and teared over.

We waited.

The group seemed to be discussing something.

Has the new boy already betrayed me? Is he talking to the uniforms now?

I listened. Nothing—just silence.

There was movement in the group, and finally we heard a loud *Jawohl* from the Ukrainian.

Silence again. We waited, motionless. Then there was a crack of bones, then hard footsteps and the sound of something being dragged toward the block in the rear.

I saw nothing; I couldn't make out a thing against the sun. My inflamed eyes kept weeping.

I listened. Nothing but a rattling noise as they threw the bodies onto the cart.

Another moment's silence, then the creak of wheels.

Not one of us made a sound, the only thing audible was the scraping of our feet as we went back into the barracks.

I'm guilty, I'm a murderer. If it hadn't been for me, it wouldn't have happened. And they'll know it was me by my voice.

The thought hit me like a blow.

Admittedly it had been dark in the barracks when I said the lethal words, none of the children had seen me, but they'd all heard me.

They'll take revenge if they recognize my voice, I thought.

If they recognize my voice, they'll betray me for a bowl of soup or a mug of water. I can't let anyone hear my voice again—anyone at all. I mustn't speak! Just keep absolutely silent. I'm a coward. A murderer. I killed the new boy. I'm scared they'll find me out. I mustn't talk anymore. I'll be an outcast, and it'll serve me right, I handed him over, I'm guilty. I'm afraid of the revenge. I knew perfectly well that children's revenge can be terrible.

I crawled into the darkness of my bunk. I felt the finality of what I'd done and the irredeemability of my guilt.

The memory flashed past me and was gone. I pushed the torn pillowcase aside and thought. Everything in the house was quiet.

Did the two new Polish kids come to look for me? Could they even recognize me? No—or yes?

If they don't hear my voice, I'm still safe. But I mustn't attract attention. They mustn't find out I came from Poland, from the camp, from the big barracks. No one must find out.

And I made lots of plans for keeping out of their way.

But after a few days they went away. I breathed again. But I had to stay on the alert.

I made no objection when I was punished for tearing the pillowcase because I didn't want anyone asking dangerous questions.

The days and weeks that followed in the orphanage were calm. I mostly sat on my own, I didn't like playing the others' games. So I had lots of time to remember.

Again and again I thought back through all my memories. I didn't want to lose or forget anything, because I wanted to run away from here, I wanted to get back, somehow. I thought the only way I'd find my way back would be if I remembered every place, every street, every house, and every barracks.

Then I compared the world I came from with the world Frau Grosz had brought me to—Frau Grosz, who'd tricked me, secretly abandoned me, and handed me over to this place.

No matter how hard I tried, I couldn't pull these two worlds together. I hunted in vain for some thread I could hold on to.

I could only get away from this unbearable strange present by going back to the world and the images of my past. Yes, they were almost as unbearable, but they were familiar, at least I understood their rules.

8

IT WAS ALREADY EVENING, and bitterly cold in the barracks. I was lying on my bunk—we were lying together in fours, squashed together to keep warm. We were almost at the front, near the entrance.

We'd hardly gone to sleep when footsteps came up to the door, it opened, and an icy wind blew in. A figure became visible. It threw in two bundles. The door was shut again.

No way to know who had thrown the bundles in at us—a uniform, a block warden, or just one of the women prisoners from the barracks next door.

The bundles were on the floor, leaning against our rack

of bunks. Cautiously I peered over the edge. The bundles moved, two heads, two white faces became visible, and huge dark eyes. They were tiny babies, they had their first teeth, but they couldn't talk yet.

Were they supposed to sleep in here with us? On the floor? I'd never seen such tiny children up close before.

I thought.

The bunks were beyond capacity already.

Maybe they'll give them somewhere to sleep tomorrow, I thought, and looked at them again.

They were moving again. They lifted their thin little arms up out of the rags and I got a shock. They were white, like their faces; only the hands and in particular the fingers were black, and I couldn't see any fingernails.

"Frozen," whispered Jankl next to me.

Cautiously we nudged them. They didn't react. They sucked on their black fingers, perhaps to warm them, I thought, and they looked off into the far distance out of big eyes, as if searching for something.

I woke up when it got light. I worked my way over to the edge of the bunk and looked down: they were still there, just like the night before, as if they hadn't moved. I leaned forward, not believing what I was seeing. Both of them were holding their hands up stiff in front of their faces, in front of their glassy, half-closed eyes. But they weren't proper hands. What I saw made no connection with anything I knew.

Their hands were black, as they were the night before, but now their fingers were white—snow-white. Except they weren't proper fingers. What I could see were tiny little white sticks that looked broken, each pointing in a different direction.

I pulled anxiously on Jankl's arm.

"What's that, Jankl—look—their hands!" I said, and Jankl took a long look over the edge of the bunk.

"Bones," he said, "just bones, that's what you look like inside, you have bones like that all over, everywhere that it feels hard. That's what holds you together, but you mustn't break them."

I touched my body, my hands, my arms, my knees. I felt the hardness, and for the first time I could picture what my bones looked like. I felt a sense of superiority, as if I'd just made a great discovery.

"But—why are those two's bones outside? I've got skin holding me together. Are they ill?" I asked, beginning to feel anxious.

Something seemed to be not right. Jankl chewed on his lip.

"Are they ill?" I asked again, and Jankl said:

"Yes, it's a sickness called hunger. Frozen fingers don't hurt. Sometime in the night they chewed their fingers down to the bone—but they're dead now."

Jankl had spoken in a quiet, soft voice, but for the first time since we'd been together, I heard something sad and bitter in his voice, and as I looked at him in surprise, I saw that he was crying.

9

JANKL WAS GOOD.

It was Jankl I had to thank for everything. If I say this, it's because I mean it quite literally.

I owe my life to Jankl. I should write a whole book in his honor, not just one pitiful little chapter. I'm ashamed, but too little has stayed in my memory.

How our friendship started in the big barracks, I don't remember either.

Jankl was already big—maybe twelve. To me, he was already a grown-up. He was always there when I needed him. He protected me, he gave me advice, he taught me a lot, he alerted me to dangers.

He showed me patiently how to tie a knot, and why this mattered.

When it got cold, he was good at wrapping my bare feet and legs in bits of cloth. Nobody knew where he got them.

"Now you tie the knots yourself," he said.

It took a lot of tries before I managed it, but he didn't get impatient, and showed me over and over again.

He reminded me of Motti.

Jankl didn't say much. He knew I didn't understand much of his strange dialect anyway. So most of the time he taught me silently, just by the way he moved his hands.

Sometimes he disappeared for long periods, and each time he came back he took me to my bunk, then carefully untied the strings he'd tied around his trouser legs at the ankles. And immediately the most unbelievable things lay between his feet: fresh potato peels, sometimes even a whole potato, or half, and sometimes a huge cabbage leaf.

He divided everything carefully, slowly, without making a sound. Then he always pushed one half over to me with a look, a mischievous smile, and a nod.

"I know all the places," he once said, and "Never get caught, or . . ." and he made a wringing movement with both hands around his neck and crossed his eyes.

I understood.

He taught me not to eat everything at one go but, whenever possible, to divide out the food over the whole day, or longer.

He taught me to hide my supplies and how to guard them.

He taught me to avoid the uniforms, and if necessary, to pick the right moment to run away from them, but only ever on his signal—and always alone, never in the same direction as everyone else, and never to scream like the other children when I was running.

But one day Jankl didn't come back.

After I'd waited a long time, I saw there was a whole crowd of agitated children outside. I went over slowly. Something must have happened, I felt afraid, but curiosity still pulled me closer. The children were standing in a semicircle and I could see that they were shrieking at each other—I could see it, but I was amazed to realize that I couldn't hear a sound—just deathly silence.

What's happened? Why can't I hear anything? Where are my ears? I've lost my ears . . .

I went even closer.

There was a grown-up standing in the middle of the semicircle, in shirtsleeves, but wearing boots. Shirtsleeves seemed to be in an absolute fury, he was yelling and pointing to a boy on the edge of the semicircle, and I saw it was Jankl.

I was panic-stricken, even though I didn't know where the danger was.

Run, Jankl, run away, I wanted to scream, but no sound came out of my throat and not a sound could get through to my ears.

Deaf and dumb and frozen to the spot, I stood there and watched.

Jankl stood there, feet together, arms and hands straight down and pressed tight to his sides, like a soldier. He stood motionless, as if turned to stone, and then—then he slowly tipped forward, still stiff, the way he'd been standing, without bending, without putting out his arms to break his fall. He fell so slowly it seemed to go on forever.

As his face hit the mud, sending up a huge spray, shirt-sleeves in the boots turned and left, and the children dispersed.

Jankl lay there peacefully, not moving.

I got down on the ground, crawled over to him, and saw his face sinking into the mud, slowly, deeper and deeper, till just his ears and the back of his head were visible.

I watched, staring at him.

Why aren't you breathing? You have to breathe, and then a bubble will come up through the mud and go plop, and then you have to lift your head, so you can breathe in again, I thought anxiously.

I wanted to touch him, take hold of him, pull his arm—whether I did or not, I don't remember.

I waited and waited—no plop came, nothing moved, his ears were now out of sight too, only a tiny bit of the back of his clean-shaven head still showed above the mud.

Two of the bigger children pushed me from behind; I looked around. They seemed to be talking to me, all upset, but I still couldn't hear a thing. I was deaf. So they took me under the arms and dragged me backward across the assembly ground.

I looked back at Jankl, getting smaller and smaller until he finally looked like any other little bump of earth between the mud puddles. As I was pulled into the barracks, I couldn't even see him anymore.

I felt absolutely helpless, crippled, I was beginning to turn freezing cold. What had happened?

I didn't understand.

All I knew was that I was alone now.

IO

I DON'T REMEMBER ANY LONGER where it was, or when. But it was one of the few days when we children were allowed out of the barracks into the open air. We jumped about, some of us crawled on the ground, others just lay there, warming themselves in the sun. In among them, a powerful, bull-necked man, who slowly took off his uniform jacket.

I'd never seen such thick, strong arms. They were astonishing.

Suddenly I can see something, there's an object the children are throwing high up in the air. It looks like a ball, but seems to be much heavier—maybe it's a wooden ball.

As I watch, it rolls between the children, they all race to pick it up and throw it again. Bull-neck watched them, his arms crossed. I'm chasing the ball too, I'd like to throw it once as well.

The ball rolls to a stop at bull-neck's feet.

The game freezes for a moment and I'm spellbound.

What's he going to do? I wonder.

He kicks the ball away with his boot. It rolls in amongst the others, and now one brave child pushes it back at bull-neck, and he shoves it back again.

The spell is broken.

He's playing with us! And as long as he's playing, he won't do anything to us.

There are several back-and-forths. We lose our shyness, and I too come closer and closer to bull-neck.

I'd like to get the ball too. I'm standing with some others right near him, and we want to catch the ball. But he's quicker. He lifts the ball into the air. We reach up our arms and hop and jump, but none of us can reach it.

I glance at the boy next to me, the little one who's leaping up with his arms high, calling, "Me, me, give it to me," with his head tilted way back to try to see the ball in bull-neck's raised hand.

The little one seems possessed.

Then I see the huge, thick arm lifting itself even higher in the air with the ball, I see the arm swung back, I see bull-neck's face suddenly grimace, then I see the arm come hurtling down in a huge swing.

I hear a strange crack—and someone beside me drops to the ground without a sound.

In disbelief and horror I stare at the little boy. His face

lies there in the sun, absolutely white, but no blood on it. I'm surprised there's no blood. But his forehead is all pushed in, there's a deep hollow in it, exactly the same size as the ball.

I keep looking down—still no blood, but I know the little one is dead.

Rage and despair explode in me, I can't think anymore.

Kill him, kill him, I'm screaming inside me, and I can see bull-neck's slack arm right above me and his self-satisfied, grinning face.

Do it like a dog—a dog! Kill him—the voice inside me screams again.

Yes—I'm a dog now, I'm a wolf.

Hands out, I take a flying leap. I grab the bare forearm, open my jaws as wide as I can, and bite with all my strength.

Harder! Deeper! You've got to kill him, I think, my jaws grinding as best they can.

Then I want to let go and run away. I loosen my hands, want to let myself drop, but my jaws won't open, they feel locked shut. They're still grinding, independent of my control. So I'm hanging from this arm by my teeth and it's pulling me upward by brute force, then coming down again, then it's carrying me away and the roaring and screaming is deafening.

Blood and spit are running down me, and my stomach begins to heave.

My memory stops at the moment when my back is slammed hard against something.

How I came out of it, I have no idea. Maybe bull-neck thought I was already dead when I hit the ground.

I I

MILA WAS SOMEWHAT OLDER than I was. I recognized her when we met each other again in the orphanage in Kraków. I didn't have to be afraid of her.

We knew each other from somewhere, from one of the many barracks probably, we weren't sure anymore, and we never talked about it.

We just looked at each other, and that was enough.

Just once, I asked her what had happened when she was taken away with her mother, and this, more or less, is what she told me:

They were already moving in the column of people who were being led from the barracks through the camp,

Mila and her mother, with uniforms in attendance, all selected to die.

It was a long way, the column kept stopping and starting, past unfamiliar barracks, and mounds of bodies, then more barracks and more mounds of bodies.

Then the column had to halt again. Mila and her mother stood still and waited.

They were standing next to a stacked pile of corpses. The SS men were patrolling impatiently up and down.

Then something completely extraordinary happened. A uniform, a young one, came slowly up beside Mila's mother, looked her up and down for a moment, then grabbed hold of her and with a single heave threw her on top of the corpses that were next to them. Mila was being held tight by her mother's hand, so she was carried along with her.

They lay there, frozen with terror, on the cold bodies. They didn't understand what had happened, or why; it had all happened so fast. But they did understand that now there was a way out.

They lay there, playing dead, absolutely still so as not to be discovered, all day until night came. Once it was dark, they slid down and mixed themselves back in among the living, but as fake living people, struck off all the lists, because they were supposed to be dead.

It was hard, because they didn't dare to be recognized either dead or alive.

Later Mila and her mother got separated after all, and neither got further news of the other.

Now Mila kept looking everywhere and asking.

———

And now we were together in this orphanage in Kraków, at least some of the time. I don't know anymore whether I lived there too, or whether I was just put there during the day, and got something to eat and was allowed to play. I was afraid of the other children, they were older than I, and their games were often cruel and dangerous. They imitated the uniforms, and were obviously practicing to be grown-ups.

If that's how it is, I don't ever want to grow up, I thought, and being with Mila gave me some sense of safety and peace.

I don't know why, but nobody ever dared come near her to do anything bad, she never got trapped into quarrels, she was untouchable.

Years later, when we were both grown up, we met quite by chance. She was working as a translator, and I'd become a musician.

Mila had managed to find her mother, and we went together to visit her—she was old by now—in a hospital. She died soon after that.

Mila and I saw each other regularly now—we often had long talks. We discussed the present, but what we really meant was our past. Both of us were living among the living, yet we didn't really belong with them—we were actually the dead, on stolen leave, accidental survivors who got left behind in life.

We loved each other, and our love was fed by our sadness. But it was always accompanied by a fear of touching what actually bound us together.

So, inevitably, we lost each other again.

12

I'M SITTING IN RAIN-SOFTENED CLAY near the door to the barracks, waiting. For what, I don't know. I watch the little streams of water. They flow past me on either side, taking strange winding paths through the mud, then they flow together again in front of me and make a bigger stream, which shimmers with the most unusual colors. I dip my forefinger into it and move it to and fro, watching the strings of color change shape and make bright whirlpools.

It's quieter these days, now that most of the children are no longer here. I don't know where they are. I can't remember where I was when they were taken away. I miss them—why didn't I go with them? Now there are only a few children in the barracks, other children, bigger and stronger. And it's not the same barracks anymore, either.

But it's the same place, same surroundings, same stink, same smoke in the air, that burns your eyes and leaves an oily deposit on your face.

The same factory stands there up on the hill, outside the fence, with the big chimney—only perhaps this one's a little smaller, a little further away, I'm not sure.

Suddenly there are lots of women here, they die in the night, then more come and they die, too.

Every morning the bodies are thrown in a pile at the corner of each barracks by the ones who are going to die during the next night.

And every morning the cart comes by, pulled by gray people in rags. They're grown-ups but they don't have any definite shape, you can't tell if they're men or women. They throw the dead women on the cart and move on again.

But the cart didn't come today, not yesterday either. The women are still lying there in a tangle. The heap is bigger than it used to be. They're lying there quite naked. I've seen it for myself—the dead ones give their clothes to the ones who are still living.

The block warden—or maybe it was the chief warden—hurries past; her stiff, high boots make the mud splash into my face. She always does that, but it's not bad. We children are just dirt, she always says, so it doesn't make any difference.

I sit here, and because there are no other children here, I go on playing with the dirt. I stir it around sometimes, to make waves in the shimmering, tinted water, and I wait to see where it will run over, and start making a colorful new canal.

Sometimes I look over at the dead women. Some of the older children have told me that little children grow in women's bellies before they're born, and I wonder: everyone keeps saying I'm so small, that must mean that I grew in a belly too. I think about my mother, I think about the one time the gray uniform took me to a woman and said:

"You can see your mother."

Does that mean all mothers have to die once they've had children?

It must be true, otherwise why would new children keep coming, and more women keep dying every night?

I look over again.

Something catches my eye, yet the mountain of corpses is just lying there, as usual. But didn't something just move over there?

That's strange. Dead women aren't allowed to move.

I look at the woman lying right on top of all the others. She's on her back, her body hanging down a little, her arms are wide open, and her breasts are tipped to one side like little sacks above her ribs, which stick out a lot, and her belly seems all swelled up.

Is my mother lying like that now?

Something *is* moving! It's the belly. I don't dare stand up, and I can't take my eyes away. I can't believe it. I inch forward cautiously on my knees. What's happening here?

"Children move inside the belly, that's how the mother

knows they want to come out," one of the older girls in the big barracks once said, once when we were still all together.

Is a child trying to come out of this belly? How is that possible? The woman's dead.

I crawl closer, I want to know.

Now I can see the whole belly. There's a big wound on one side, with something moving in it. I get to my feet, so that I can see better. I poke my head forward, and at this very moment the wound springs open, the wall of the stomach lifts back, and a huge, blood-smeared, shining rat darts down the mound of corpses. Other rats run startled out of the confusion of bodies, heading for open ground.

I saw it, I saw it! The dead women are giving birth to rats!

Rats—they're the deadly enemies of the little children in the camp. Rats that attack us at night, that bite us, leaving painful wounds that never heal, that nobody knows how to heal, and that make the children's living bodies start to rot away.

"Mother, mama, my mama, what have you done?"

I open my mouth to scream, in shock and fear, but nothing comes out of my throat. It feels as if my gullet is being squashed into my chest, and I hear a noise deep inside me, a sort of ringing and crackling, like something fragile being stepped on. Then there's a long silence.

After a time I try to get up. My mind is empty, I've forgotten everything. I don't know who I am. Who am I?

I touch my legs again and again. I undo the rags

around my calves and feel the skin. Is it skin, or do I actually have gray fur? Am I a rat or a human? I'm a child—but am I a human child or a rat child, or can you be both at once?

Still staring at the women, I kneel in the mud with my mouth open, and I can't close it.

Everything inside me comes loose and seems to flow away; I flow away along with my blood and vomit in the bright, muddy runnels of water, down the street of the camp to wherever the runnels peter out.

Nothing connects to anything else anymore. Nothing is in its right place. Nothing has any value.

Is this what it's like to die? Am I dying?

There are no feelings left. I can't feel if I'm breathing, I can't feel my ever-present hunger, or thirst.

I'm just an eye, taking in what it sees, giving nothing back.

But I'm cold.

Many years later I went with my wife for the birth of our first son. I wanted to be there with her, to support her.

The first thing that slowly became visible was the half-round of the baby's head. As a first-time father, I didn't know how much dark hair a newborn baby can have. I wasn't ready for this little half-head of hair. All I could do was stand still and stare at it, and once again, like an echo from before, I heard the ringing and crackling noise in my chest.

I must have looked pretty bad as I left the birthing room. I walked down the long corridor, past the open dayroom where the nursing sisters were sitting having coffee and eyeing me curiously and giggling.

As I went out into the open air, their mocking commentary still rang in my ears.

They had been murmuring something about men—and weaklings who had no stomach for things.

13

THE MORNING ROUTINE OF STANDING, counting, and having the roll called had gone on longer than usual. I no longer remember how it came about, but I found myself in a group that was going "on the transport." That's what they said.

Anxious about the unusual alteration in the day's routine, I found myself almost immediately standing in a car so packed with people that I couldn't move, or see out. I'm not even sure whether it was a truck or a railcar. Such dizziness came over me that I couldn't make out anything much—at some point I must have gone to sleep.

All I remember is the end of the journey, and the

memory is full of holes, muddled, in broken pictures with no order to them, too many pieces missing.

A terrible noise startles me awake, jerking me back into consciousness. I am hemmed in between grown-ups; I'm shaken, pushed, shoved. I can't see a thing. Above the general din there's a constant overriding yelling and screaming from what sounds like a thousand people.

What's happened? All I can see is legs and stomachs, none of them with any idea that I'm down here, that I don't want to be trampled, that I need air. With enormous effort, I manage to get my arms up, so that I can put them over my face. The sharp elbows take effect. I can breathe a little.

But the pressure starts getting worse again right away. People keep leaning more and more to the side, and over me.

Where are we? Are we still in the car? Is the car tipping over and taking us with it?

I'm hot. The pressure becomes unendurable. It's stopping me from breathing. Then suddenly I'm not inhaling air anymore, it's smoke, and the smoke is getting stronger.

Where am I? I have to get out of here. Is the car on fire? I'm suffocating! There's fire somewhere, and we're burning up!

Panic seizes me.

Why is everyone wedged so tight together? Why aren't they moving? Why don't they notice that we're on fire? Why doesn't anyone open the car? Are we still in the car? Do something!

Nothing moves, everything has turned still, the noise has stopped, the screaming has died down. Only now do I see that the legs and backs and stomachs that pen me in are naked. I'm amazed.

Suddenly in front of me a glimmer of light, something opens, there's a little air.

That must be the way out, I think, and:

Why isn't anyone getting out? Why isn't anyone making space? I want to get out—I don't want to burn up!

With a wild fury that I've never felt in myself before, I begin to struggle and kick, to make a space for myself, and then I draw breath, deeper than I've ever drawn breath before, and I begin to scream with all my strength as I've never screamed before.

At this very moment, like an answer to my great long scream, something behind me moves. Two big, strong hands seize me under the arms. They throw me forward, up over everyone else, to where the light is, and air. I fly out over the motionless bodies, fall to earth somewhere.

I'm in the open air, I can see the sky.

What happened? Have I been lying here long? I wake up as if from an anesthetic. I look around:

Behind me, a great high shadow, maybe the car that brought us here.

In front of me a steep embankment that stands lit up by the sun with a straight, sharp edge against the sky. All around people are lying, lots of them, nobody moving, nobody to help me, they all look dead.

Why are they so naked? Some of them all naked, others

half-naked. When did they get undressed? And why? It's not hot out here, I think, puzzled again.

Something terrible has happened, but I don't know what. I want to get away from here. I'm afraid. I want to go up there, where the sun's shining, out of this shadow. I look up again.

Up on the edge, something moves: I make out the shape of a man, waving and calling. Then he starts running to and fro. His waving gets more urgent.

There are dead bodies on the embankment, too. But now one of them begins to move, slowly at first, and timidly. Then he starts flailing his arms and legs; he climbs up to the other man who's still standing up there, waving.

Like a beetle up a wall, I think.

Carefully I work my way over the bodies to where the embankment begins. I want to get up to the two men standing in the sun. They've seen me, they're calling and yelling, and now both of them are waving, I'm to come up as quickly as possible.

The slope is steep and full of loose earth. I try to hold on to scattered clumps of grass to pull myself up, but I slide backward more than once. The clumps don't hold. I don't understand, they don't seem to have taken root. So I have to hang on to the arms and legs of the corpses on the slope. Slowly I work my way up again.

If only they hold, and don't come crashing down with me, the way the clumps of grass did . . .

I fight down panic and a feeling that I'm going to faint. I'm almost at the top, I can almost see over the ridge already. My legs are shaking and they ache. I start to tremble, I lose my balance.

Off at an angle below me, there's a big man lying as if he'd been hung up on the wall like a picture, his huge bare stomach a shiny white in the sun.

He's all there is between me and falling. I have to put my bare feet on his stomach for support. But I don't want to—I'll hurt him. And if he starts to slide, and takes me with him, he could squash me, is what flashes through my head.

Then I tread, or rather jump, onto the big white stomach. My foot sinks right down in it. I go up and down and sway as if I'm on a seesaw, but the corpse doesn't fall. I begin to retch, I want to be sick, but I can't, my stomach's empty.

With one last effort I drag myself up over the edge of the embankment. My hands get a firm grip. I pull myself forward on my stomach, until only my legs are swinging over the void.

I've done something terrible, I think. I trod on a dead man. He couldn't defend himself. Can dead people feel pain? The dead man saved me, and I wanted to be sick on him.

I feel guilty. Can a dead person forgive you?

Slowly I realize that what I'm lying on up here is a railway embankment. My hands are holding tight to a rail. I wait, exhausted, my mind's a blank. I have no strength left.

After a while I turn myself around carefully and look back. I see the bodies I climbed over, lying as if glued to the steep slope. Looking further back, back over the car, I can see the place where I was thrown by the big hands. Those bodies here. I can't count them, there are too many. They're lying every which way. There's still smoke in the air, my eyes smart, and the smell makes me sick.

A little further away I see the vague shapes of what seem to be three railcars. They're standing off-center, slightly crazily, not in a straight line.

What is all this? Did we come in these cars? And why are they down there in the field and not up here on the embankment, on their rails? I lie down again on the railbed.

To my right there are people running along the embankment, four or five of them. Some are already a long way away, but I can still hear them yelling. They all seem to be running in the one direction, as if they know where they're going. They keep pointing, yelling again, waving their arms in the air, gesturing urgently in the same direction they're running.

Then I look left.

At first all I see is smoke and empty space. The tracks end right next to where I am, the embankment stops abruptly, like the end of a military fortification. My eyes are burning and watering. I look over the edge into the bottom of the trench, then out over it. I can't understand what I'm seeing through the billows of smoke, and at the same time I do understand, but it doesn't connect up with anything I know, either in pictures or in words. I just feel that this is a place where everything ends, not just the embankment and the rails. This is where this world stops being a world at all.

Someone's yelling:

"Come on, get up, come back here—now!"

I put my head on my arm and look down at the pebbles between the rails. I don't care, I don't want to hear. They can yell and run around, but leave me alone. I've had enough, I can't anymore.

My legs seem to be dead, I can't feel them anymore. That means I can't run anyhow, and there's nowhere I want to run.

All that seems to be left of me is my eyes, my head, and two hands holding on. I want to go to sleep, just to sleep, nothing else.

For a moment, everything is quiet.

Then suddenly there's more yelling, this time right up close to my ear. I see a lot of legs standing around me. There's a woman. She bends over, she wants me to get up and come with them now, quickly, to the right, where the others are running along the embankment and are already all small in the distance.

For the first time, I consciously refuse. I don't want to obey anyone ever again. I shake my head, I don't know where my legs are, I just want to sleep, I want to be left in peace, I don't want to do what everyone else does anymore, I've had enough.

The confusion of voices over my head won't stop. Why don't the grown-ups understand? I don't need them anymore. There are no more questions, I know everything now—I've already looked out over the end of the world.

The woman is yelling at me, she's very angry, and afraid, and impatient. The others are yelling, too, I have to run, with them, now, before it's too late.

The woman bends over me again. She's screaming at me, and I feel her spit. I think she's going to slap my face. She hauls me up by the wrist. She's rough and very angry.

So they simply drag me away with them, my numb feet trailing in the gravel. They run.

I can't, I cry with fury. I just fall down, I'm picked up again, this time by both wrists, so I'm being carried rather than running of my own accord.

This forced march went on and on and on. On my right, the sun was already going down over the plain like a fireball that etched itself like burning acid into my inflamed eyes. I could hardly see where I was going.

Gradually the pace eased off into an endless monotonous trot. The only time it was interrupted was when two or three people came running across the fields. A farmer's wife waved a basket at us, and after that my memory just turns into a long gray fog.

It wasn't till long afterward, when it had turned cold and the first snow was falling, that my mind began to work again, and I became aware of my surroundings.

The world was full of barracks again, there was another block warden and a chief warden. But now it was more often men who guarded us. Men who did nothing but yell, and sometimes hit us, and also sometimes took away other children and didn't bring them back again.

For the first time, however, the thirst wasn't as bad as the hunger whenever I could push a handful of snow into my mouth without being seen.

The place was always crowded to bursting, and the air was often full of smoke. I knew that smell.

I had my usual barracks again, like before, but this one seemed to be in a different place.

Who brought my barracks here? And why?

This one wasn't at the top of a slope anymore. And the enormous chimney was no longer up there on the hill, where the barracks ended and the big fence began. There was no more hill. Here everything was as flat as a plate.

And here the barracks streets went on forever, far further than I could see.

Maybe, no, not just maybe, they go right to the end of the world, to the edge of the plate, and nobody here knows what it's like there.

"What's it like?" I demanded of a big boy who was next to me. I knew. But he didn't know. He didn't say anything, just stared up at the sky.

14

I'D LOST ALL SENSE of place a long time ago. It was a long time since I'd been in Majdan Lublin, in Majdanek. The barracks all around me were different, they kept on changing, yet they were always the same, sometimes the place changed too, I don't know anymore. But my barracks always stayed the same, it seemed to follow me everywhere.

Outside the big fence, there was nothing anymore, just flat fields and a pale wood, which was mostly covered in mist.

There were always new children around me. I could almost never understand what they were saying, and even less from the grown-ups. Everything seemed to be dissolving, murky, a blur. I didn't know enough to make sense of it, the constant changes confused me. The days suddenly had no set order, none of the regular timetable they'd had before. There didn't seem to be any rules anymore. I have some shreds of memory still, like a brief flash of light, but their meaning is much less clear.

For a time I wasn't allowed out of the barracks. I didn't know why. When it was time for roll call and everyone hurried outside, I was forbidden to go too. Each time someone grabbed hold of me and pushed me into a corner, or maybe it was a hole. A cover was put over me, and then a plank, and I wasn't supposed to move. I struggled, I didn't understand why they wouldn't let me, I didn't want to be left alone. I was afraid and began to cry.

A slap took care of that.

It went on that way for quite a long time, day after day, every morning and every evening. Everyone who lived in the barracks ran outside, two grown-ups stayed with me, I got the slap, then the cover, then the plank, then the two of them ran out as well; I knew it was them by the sound of their wooden clogs.

Another time a group of women took me outside with them. We ran past a jumble of unfamiliar barracks and lots of unknown faces.

Suddenly we were in a column, we had to wait, and one of the women made a sign for me to hold on tight to her leg. Then she spread her skirt over me. We waited like that for a time, and then began to move on again.

It went on for a long time and it was freezing cold.

Eventually they brought me into a room that was quite different from any room I knew.

This room was big and high and had a window on one wall. Against each of the other three walls a huge pile of pieces of cloth, rags, maybe clothes, towered all the way up to the roof. Right in front of the middle pile, opposite the window, there was a table.

Two women were standing barefoot at the table. One of them was throwing clothes or rags from one of the piles, and the other turned them this way and that, and took them away again.

I was pushed through under the table to the foot of the mountain of clothes. Hands groped around in the mountain, hollowed out a nest, and I crawled into it. This was my new home. I liked the quiet in the room. I liked the strange soapy smell and the unaccustomed warmth. There were only three or four women there by day. They talked to each other quietly, they were friendly, and they made signs that I wasn't allowed to speak or call out to them, that I was safe as long as I stayed in my burrow under the mountain.

Once a day, I was allowed to crawl out. Each time there was a tin bowl standing ready on the edge of the table, at eye height. I pulled the spoon out of my clothes and began to eat. This spoon was my single most precious possession, and I'd carried it and a mug on a chain under my shirt for a long time now.

Then one of the women would prepare a cloth under the table, for me to relieve myself on. Then I crawled back into my cozy burrow, the woman bundled up the cloth and took it away. This happened every day, always the same. Was it a few days, a few weeks, a month, longer? I have no idea.

But the last day in the room is embedded in sharp contours in my mind, indelibly.

The women came as they always did, just before dawn. As always, I heard their whispered conversation, their footsteps, the rustling of material and clothing as they sorted them out. As always, the tin bowl stood ready and the cloth was under the table.

I was long gone back under the mountain of rags when I was startled by loud, hard footsteps, loud, deep men's voices, and terrified cries from the women. I inched forward and spied through the cloths. I saw the legs of the table, and between me and the table the hem of a skirt, two bare legs and feet. Very carefully I looked between the legs out into the room.

The loud men's voices and the noise of boots were now mixed in with high screams that were getting louder and louder. I saw pairs of black boots and naked legs running this way and that. Suddenly, the screaming died away into a soft whimpering, the sound of boots slowed down but got more threatening, the noise subsided—I peered out and listened as intently as I could.

The boots all came to stand together in front of the mountain of clothes on the right-hand wall. It was quiet for a moment, then I was absolutely amazed to hear the shrill cries of children. There must have been several of them, including big ones.

The boots and bare feet started to run again.

Other children in here? I couldn't believe it. I was sure I'd been alone.

The crying of the children, the women's screams, and the men's yelling mingled with the thumping and trampling until it filled the room. A full hunt seemed to be under way. I heard blows and dragging sounds that got further away. Then it got quiet again. I slid further forward, lifted a few more of the cloths away from my face and looked out again under the table legs to where the bare calves were still standing, only now they were closer to me.

I saw the room, I saw the open window opposite. Outside the window, the shapes of men swinging something—weapons or sticks—through the air. Inside, over to my right, in front of the other mountain of clothes, several pairs of boots still standing.

Uniform jackets, bending over, came into my field of vision; arms were stirring through the bottom of the mountain almost directly opposite me.

Two small, wriggling bundles were pulled out by large hands; the noise got louder again, more yelling from the boots, then a big swing and the bundles flew clear across the room, all spread out in the strangest way as if they were trying to flap their wings, through the window, and out.

Silence for a second—and in the silence, from outside, twice over the unmistakable sound of breaking skulls.

The calves in front of me moved, a bare foot came up, set itself against my face, and shoved me hard back into my burrow. The foot stayed there for a bit, squashing my nose and mouth together. I struggled for air. Then the foot was lifted away and I drew breath as carefully as I could. I could hear the echoing stamp of boots and the thud of bare feet slowly going away until there was no more sound.

Deathly silence. The storm seemed to have passed as quickly as it had come. It was only now that I felt any fear. I waited and listened for what seemed like forever. The room appeared to be empty.

It must have been late afternoon when the door opened and quiet footsteps approached. I heard whispering.

The rags over my head parted and women's arms reached around carefully for me. A woman's head, all shaved, bent down, kissed me, and I was lifted up out of my burrow with a smile and a sigh. Two more women were standing in the room. They looked at me questioningly, in disbelief. They shook their shaved heads slowly, went "tz-tz-tz," but they were smiling too.

The biggest woman began saying something to me quickly and urgently. All I understood was that we had to get out of the room and this barracks as fast and as quietly as possible, without being seen, that she would go first, that I had to do everything she did, and that we had to go out one by one, past the house, past the window, then run behind the barracks next door. She'd be waiting there.

We stood in a row behind the doors leading to the outside, and listened. The big one was in front, the others behind me. We peered out and waited. It was getting dark, it was foggy and raining. There were patches of snow.

The big woman set off at a run. I stuck my head out, looked left down the wall in the direction she'd taken. She'd already passed the window, now she disappeared around the corner.

"Don't worry—quick—now!" said an urgent whisper behind me.

But I was frightened, really frightened, I clung tight

to the door frame. But my hands were pulled loose and I was given a gentle push.

Now I started to run too, as fast as I could, the length of the barracks wall, with a concentration born of terror.

Don't fall, don't stumble now—falling would be disaster, I thought, with my eyes fixed on where I had to go.

Then everything in me froze, turned into a single enlarged moment of time:

What I saw on the ground, up against the wall, was the two bundles, still lying there, or rather, what was left of them. The pieces of cloth were undone, lay around all torn, and in amongst them the babies on their backs, arms and legs outspread, stomachs all swollen and blue. And where once their little faces must have been, a red mess mixed with snow and mud.

Nothing else to see—except the skulls were smashed open.

A mass of yellow, sticky-shiny stuff had flowed out and was splashed against the wall, on the ground, and right across the path I had to follow. My stomach heaved with horror and disgust.

Can I jump over, without treading in the yellow stuff, or slipping in it and falling down?

I mustn't fall down. If I jump and fall, that's it. A block warden might hear, or a chief warden—it would all be over. I have to get past—I just have to jump.

I fought to stop my legs seizing up, fought to keep the moment from freezing me there for all eternity. It seemed to take forever until I was over the bodies and past them, and I felt all alone.

Who was there to help? I could hardly feel my legs any-more. They seemed to have solidified into shapeless lumps. I ran and ran, for hours it seemed, until I reached the corner and saw, between the next barracks, almost invisi-ble in the fog, the shadow of the big woman waiting for me.

I've never been able to free myself of this picture, or of any of the others. They came back again and again, still do today—and this one in particular.

In the orphanage in Switzerland, there was also a room for nursing babies and little children. I once found myself in there by accident. When I saw the babies, it all came back, the numbing, crippling, freezing sensation that crept up from my feet, up past my knees, into my thighs and up against my innards. I slipped out cautiously, and never once went into that room again.

I still feel it today, whenever I catch sight of very small children, feel myself tensing to jump over the two bun-dles. I see them clearly. I see them vanish from under me as I fly over them with my legs stretched wide, as if in slow motion. In such dreadful slow motion that I think I'm going to fall right onto them.

I often reproach myself, I can't understand how I could have felt nothing for the little ones back then. Although I was just a child myself, was I already so brutalized that there was nothing left in me, no sympathy, no pity, not even anger?

Because I felt nothing then, nothing but disgust and my own icy terror.

15

CHILDREN WERE BEING taken away again every day, as so often before. We were just a little group now, maybe ten or twelve of us.

The interior of the barracks was now divided in two. One part was for us, in the other were women, who sometimes appeared like shadows out of the darkness, took care of us, then disappeared again behind hanging pieces of cloth into their territory.

Lots of the bunks stayed empty; we were colder than before. I didn't understand what was happening. I couldn't understand the remaining children, either; they spoke languages I didn't know. I hardly took them in at all—except for one child, that is, I can remember something about that one. I'm not sure if it was a boy or a girl. This one was older than I, perhaps, and called something like Kobo, or Kola or Kala—I'm not sure anymore. He or she seemed to be the favorite of the others, and I remember a round head on a long, thin neck. He/she liked to play and make faces, and sometimes even laughed.

But one day, I noticed that Kobo had vanished, along with the others.

Why have I been left on my own? Have I missed something again, or slept through something? Why am I always the last to see what's going on? It felt bad.

I didn't know what to do. The unaccustomed silence in the barracks was unsettling, everything around me seemed to be dissolving into inexplicable disorder.

I saw people going away, crowds of them. Most of them seemed to be going however they chose, not in step and not in the usual column. Most of them seemed to know where they were going; they didn't turn around as they went past, nobody paid any attention to me, and I watched them go until they were swallowed up in the sea of barracks.

Despair grew and grew.

They're all going off somewhere, they all seem to know something I don't know. Why am I always the only one who doesn't understand? Why doesn't someone tell me? Where are they all going? I don't have anywhere to go, I'm hungry and I'm freezing cold.

There were only three or four women left in my barracks. They didn't say anything, just silently passed me something to eat now and then.

There were no orders, no rules to define the day the

way it was before, no roll call, nobody bothered. The block warden seemed to have disappeared, no chief warden came by anymore, even the big men in the fancy uniforms stayed away, the ones who used to look for children and take them away.

Then, all at once, I felt the silence. No orders being given, no yelling, no crying, no standing still in rows in the morning and at night; the indistinguishable tumult of voices that used to fill the air had gone quiet. I stayed where I was and spent the days half-asleep.

I was shocked out of my daze only once. There was a fire somewhere, barracks were burning down, but it didn't worry me for long. I didn't care. I went back to sleep. I was tired.

But there's one morning I do remember, as clear as glass. I was standing outside, in the cold. I was waiting at the corner of one of the neighboring barracks, looking down the street of the camp. I don't know what I was waiting for, and why I was standing in the cold. I scratched a hole in the slushy ground so that I could put my feet into the mud, which was warmer. In the distance I heard shots, lots at first, then not so many; they didn't come any nearer, and I stopped being afraid, and stayed where I was.

Again I saw people I'd never seen before. Most of them weren't in orderly rows, most of them went by in a confusing, disorganized mob. There were women, sometimes men too, and sometimes big children, but I didn't know them. They all came from the same direction. They turned ahead of me into a side street and disappeared between the barracks toward the horizon, the end of world.

For a long time, all morning maybe, I froze and
watched the puzzling activity, and I saw that the women
from my barracks were also joining one of the groups, and
then they slowly disappeared out of my view. They
walked slowly through the rows of barracks toward the
wires, to the fence, where it was forbidden to go.

What do they all want there? That's where the world
ends, there's nowhere further to go. What should I do? I
just waited, without any idea, without knowing what
I was waiting for.

Then another group came. Women, a few children, a
very few men, and they turned off in front of me, just like
the others. I looked after them. A few rays of sun broke
through and began to warm me.

Then suddenly, the group comes to a halt. One of the
women turns around, detaches herself from the knot of
people, runs back along the path, and she's screaming.
She throws her arms up in the air so wildly that her rags
slip off and you can see her white breast. But she doesn't
notice, she keeps waving and calling and calling and her
voice is falling over itself:

"Binjamin," she's screaming. "Binjamin, oy Binjamin," and she keeps running in my direction.

Spellbound, I stare at her. What's the matter with her?
She's quite close to me now.

"Binjamin—is it you?" she calls again, all excited, her
whole voice like a question.

Suddenly it hits me—I'm the person she's calling, I *am* Binjamin, she means me. I'd almost forgotten that I have a name.

The woman bends over me, I look up into a round face that seems to be saying "You—here?" as she stares disbelievingly at me.

"Binjamin, Binjamin," she keeps panting, and hugs me so tight it hurts. What does it mean? Who is she? It doesn't make any sense to me, all I do know is that I *am* Binjamin, that she does mean me, but I have no idea who she is, I don't remember her at all.

"Come with me, come quick, before anyone sees you here," she gasps and pulls me toward the waiting group at a run.

What's happening? Why do I have to leave? Why can't I just stay here? I've been standing here all morning. I'm hungry. Will she give me something to eat?

I'm too tired to ask, I just let it all happen. The shapes in the group take me into the middle as we move on, so I get only glimpses of where we're going.

We pass through row after row of unfamiliar barracks, where I've never been before. Near a cross street and a passage between the fences, there's an open gate. We come to a halt.

Another surprise: just next to a barracks I see a group of women half-dressed, naked almost, washing themselves out in the open air—in spite of the cold. They stand barefoot in a big puddle of water, snow, and muck, looking after us without saying a word.

After a brief pause we follow the passage between the

fences, and then we're on an even bigger street. As we get closer and closer to the outer fence, I begin to get suspicious; it's what the other children call the End of the World.

The thought terrifies me—we're not on our way to a new barracks, or looking for food: we're actually going to go to the other side, outside the big fence, out of this world. Over there, in the fields, there's nothing anymore, there was a world once, but it disappeared long ago, the older children always said so. But how can you go somewhere that's disappeared, that no longer exists? There's nothing out there on the other side of the fence—everything came to an end out there. As I keep thinking this, my anxiety rises. We're doing something that's impossible. Or does this actually mean we're going out there to die? Is this we're doing now what the big children called "the death walk"?

In spite of the cold, I'm sweating.

We're almost at the fence, close to the last buildings. A uniform is standing by the side of the road. The group slows its pace. We go by. He doesn't do a thing. He doesn't shoot. He doesn't yell. He just turns around with both hands in his pockets and stares wordlessly after us.

I can't make out what they're saying in the group, but the voices get louder and more excited as we pass the fence, go through the gate and out into the open country.

I'm dead tired, my legs feel dull and numb again, as if they don't belong to me, just my knees ache. But the unknown woman who knows my name pulls me along relentlessly. When do I get to die? Why does she go on hurting me? I can't feel my feet anymore. I stumble. I fall. I lie with my face in the snow, beating the frozen ground with my fists.

There's nothing here anymore, nothing, just fields and fog. No barracks to sleep in, nothing left to eat. We're on our way to nothing, it's all over, the world's over. I've left it! I can't go back, I'll starve, it's the end now. I want to go to sleep—leave me alone! I'm not hungry anymore, I don't want to see anyone ever again, I want to be alone, I just want it all to stop, I want to go to sleep.

My memory stops here; maybe I really did fall asleep.

The next thing I have any recollection of was months later, and even that is hazy. The unknown woman who knew my name kept me with her. We walked for a very long time, sometimes we ran, sometimes we sat on a horse-drawn cart. After a long time we came to a small town high up on a mountain. The strange woman who knew me had been talking for days about Sandomierz and how we absolutely had to get there—just for a few days, she said. I understood that it was something to do with papers that she had to arrange.

During the day, she locked me in the tiny attic room where we lived. She left in the early morning, always carrying lots of printed and handwritten papers. She was away all day.

It was a good time. I sat for hours on the window ledge, looking out. I could see way down to the flat land under the cliffs at Sandomierz and to the river, glittering between the trees. It was spring already, the snow had melted, and I watched all the birds flying over the valley and the river below me. I daydreamed about flying with them, soundless and free.

"We have to go back to Kraków now—it's all settled," she said one night.

Back? To Kraków? Isn't that where we were to begin with, after we went through the big fence? I brooded about it, I wasn't sure of myself, I didn't dare ask questions, I didn't even want to try; I didn't talk anyway.

Nothing has stayed with me about the journey to Kraków. On the other hand, I retraced the route from the station to the Miodowa synagogue like a sleepwalker twenty years later, the first time I ever went back to the city.

For several days we kept going back and waiting in front of this synagogue. The woman who knew me wanted to speak to someone, she said it was about me, that she was going to "deliver" me here.

At last the huge doors opened. An impressive-looking man in a long black coat and a big black hat looked down at me and smiled. The woman spoke to him vehemently. I only understood the first words she said.

"I'm bringing you the little Wilkomirski boy, Binjamin Wilkomirski." She took me by the shoulders and pushed me forward, so that he could see me better. He nodded.

I was very surprised and proud that I now had two names. The woman kept talking. The rabbi's face turned serious, then he smiled at me, then turned serious again. I began to trust him. I felt he belonged with us, that he was one of the barracks people too.

He took my hand, led me into the garden behind the

synagogue and up some stone steps at the back of the house, to a sort of balcony or arcade. His hand was firm and felt good, it didn't grab or push. It said things, it comforted and calmed and conveyed safety. Since the time of Motti, and then Jankl, I hadn't felt a hand like that.

Up on the balcony there were two older men sitting at a table, and they had black hats, too. They had papers in front of them. The rabbi went away, and the two men inspected me.

They began to ask questions, lots of questions, but I don't know what they were anymore. All I do know is that, without knowing how, I suddenly began to talk in a way I'd never talked before. I heard myself talking, as if it was someone else inside me. I talked like a waterfall, but I have no idea anymore what I said. But at some point it was enough, there was only a sick feeling in my throat, I stopped talking and everything inside me was quiet again, the way it was before.

The two men got up in a hurry and went away. One of them came back after a time; he looked different, there were drops of water still hanging in his beard and his face was a sort of gray green color.

Looking straight in front of him and not at me, and without saying another word, he took me down the stone stairs again into the garden.

"Wait in front of the entrance, you're going to be collected," said the rabbi, who'd come back to meet me down there. He stroked my shoulder and back, which made a great impression on me, then he disappeared.

Where was the woman who knew my name? She'd gone—I never saw her again.

Where they took me, and who took me—I've no idea. It's all a blur.

Sometimes I was with lots of children, then with just a handful—probably I kept moving from one place to another. I do know that I kept running away, that I wanted to find my barracks, where I belonged.

The city, other people, other children, all put me in a panic. A tangle of questions kept gnawing at my brain like acid, tormenting me more and more, sometimes flooding my head like molten lead. I couldn't say the questions out loud, they choked my throat and mouth and set my heart racing, or else threatened to make it stop altogether; I couldn't get anything out, so there was no hope of any answer.

What kind of people are these? A lot of them have strange uniforms, different ones. They're all nicely dressed, they live in whole houses, which are warm, and not in ruins or in barracks. I don't belong with them.

The people who live in whole houses and don't wear striped shirts and have everything to eat, as much as they want, they're the ones who kill the others. They're the ones I have to fear, the ones with fat faces and strong arms and legs and terrible big hands. They're the ones who sometimes grab children and take them away and throw them into the fire, so as to make room for new children.

I don't want to live with these people! What are they planning? Where's my barracks?

I can hardly believe what the grown-ups and a lot of the children have to say—according to them, the city isn't new. It was always here, even during the time I was in the barracks. The city and the world outside the fence didn't disappear, the way I was told. Some of the children say they were never in a barracks, and that they've lived here for a long time. Lots of them also say that they hid outside the fence in other places that didn't disappear.

Others say they're going to wait until they're picked up by papa, or mama, or their older brothers and sisters.

My mama's dead.

Oh God—I had brothers too once, I did—I remember now. Where are they?

My brothers will come and get me out of this city where the murderers live—where are Motti and Daniel? Why don't they come now, before it's too late?

But then, why weren't we all together in the barracks behind the big fence? Why me? Why Jankl? Why did they tell me the world outside the fence had disappeared, and that it was better to live in the barracks than to be thrown in the fire? Why were the other children thrown in the fire? Why didn't they get to me? Did they forget me? Or are they still waiting? What will they do when they find me?

Why are there even children who say they never had to hide at all?

Something here doesn't make sense—they've tricked me. They've all tricked me. Maybe I didn't need to live behind the fence at all. Or Jankl either. But Jankl's dead.

Was it all about nothing?

Now I have warm clothes and hot food. That's nice. But I'm living with cheats and murderers! And the grown-ups all lied to me. Best not to listen to them ever again.

Not even Mila can give me the answers. She's the only one I'd believe. But she only knows what I do.

Wouldn't it be better for me to get back to the barracks, before anyone notices that I'm here in the city, still alive? But where is my barracks? They took it away. Here there's nothing but stone houses—everywhere—and no grandpa, no mama, no brother to take me away. Where can I go, what can I do?

Many years later I recognized some of the streets in Kraków again: Miodowa Street and its synagogue in the Jewish quarter. The Dluga and Paulinska Street. The house on Augustianska Street with the big staircase and the exercise bars in the playground.

The faces of Mischia and Olga resurface; they used to take us for walks. I also recognized Jozefinska Street and the Limanovskiego, which oddly are somewhere else entirely, namely Podgorze, the ghetto area built by the Nazis, on the other side of the Vistula. I begged there once. Number 38, Zamoiskiego also comes back to me—what was there? Nowadays there's a new building on the site.

I remember that I begged on the streets every time I ran away from somewhere, and that it was hard, because the bigger children savagely defended the best begging places.

I also remember a Purim festival, more precisely I just remember the bit about "killing Haman." Lots of children were sitting squashed around a long table by candlelight. I beat with my stick as hard as I could, and didn't want to stop, until two soft hands took hold of my arms from behind, and a voice spoke to me soothingly.

Then suddenly, I think it was already autumn, and cool, a house, almost empty rooms, iron bedsteads. Sudden uproar in the house. Children running to the windows, me too. We leaned over the windowsills and looked down into the street. A deafening racket rose up at us, coming from a black mass of stamping, yelling people surging through the street. They were swinging planks and sticks through the air and roaring like drunkards. A warning memory took hold of me and I climbed down from the windowsill and went to hide in the corner behind an open door. I heard grown-ups' voices, very upset; in the house, someone called:

"They're killing Jews again."

It wasn't long after that when Frau Grosz appeared and asked me:

"Do you want to come? I'll say—you must say that you're my son, that way I can take you with me," and:

"Switzerland is a beautiful country."

16

I WAS STANDING WAITING, staring at the rails and streaming sweat. A children's nurse from the Swiss orphanage had brought me here to the station of the nearest town. She was holding tight to my sleeve, in case I ran away.

There had been a terrible row before that, in the orphanage. A strange woman had visited the day before, and had a long talk with the director of the home; a doctor was there too. He examined me, wrote lots of things down on a piece of paper, nodded, and said:

"In a few days this lady will fetch you, you're going to live with her, you're getting foster parents." And then, turning to the strange lady, he said:

"And what have you thought about transport?"

And the strange lady said:

"I think we'll take the train."

I didn't listen to another word; I began to scream and yell, I jumped at the strange lady, hit her with my fists in a frenzy of rage and fear, and ran away before anyone could catch me. It was the beginning of a wild hunt through the building, and they overpowered me. Biting, kicking, hitting—none of it was any use, they had an iron grip on me. It was the first time I was ever hit in this house—for my "appalling behavior," they said.

"No, no transport, no—I won't go on any transport," I screamed despairingly. "I want to go home, let me go home. Not the transport, please!"

Lots of people talked to me but I didn't understand what they said—I didn't want to understand anything. They would only lie to me, like the gray uniforms who took me from the railway station before.

They tried to give the word "transport" other names, but I didn't let myself be fooled. After all, I knew the word from personal experience and from what lots of children had told me. Whenever I asked them about their parents or brothers or sisters, it was always the same:

"They were put on the transport."

And that always meant they'd gone forever. Almost nobody ever came back who'd been on a "transport."

I was forced to recognize that running away was impossible; my transport was already "written down," as they said.

I lost all hope in the days that were left. I had to stay in the house. I was constantly watched; they ran to lock doors behind me and in front of me, so that I wouldn't get away from them at the last moment.

And now I was standing here on the platform of a little town in Switzerland, waiting for my transport. The nurse was holding me by the wrist now, because I was making fists; I didn't want to give her my hand.

The train pulled in, the strange lady got out, all that changed was the hand holding my wrist. We waited in silence, another train came, and we went to the place where the strange lady lived.

It was a big house, in a big garden, and there weren't any other children. But the husband of the strange lady was there. He greeted me with a rather awkward smile. Apart from him, there didn't seem to be anybody in the house.

It was evening already, they gave me food, nothing I knew; absolutely everything was unfamiliar. The food took a whole series of strange journeys: first it was in a frying pan, then it was in a bowl, then it was on a plate that got put on another plate. This all happened with three different frying pans, three bowls and plates, and then yet another plate, separate, that one was only for uncooked vegetables—I had to eat salad, they said, it was healthy. It tasted so sour that my stomach went tight. At the end I sat bewildered in front of a reddish yellow ball that was put in front of me on another new plate. Why all the new plates? This was the fourth already.

"Don't you like oranges?" they asked, and I shrugged my shoulders. I didn't know what they meant.

The man took the ball, peeled it, and divided it into slices. I almost choked when I swallowed the slice without chewing.

Then it was time to sleep. Some doors were opened.

"This is your room," they said, and the man went away. The room was enormous, and the idea of sleeping there alone without any other children next to me was frightening.

I lay down on the bed.

"Now you must learn to say 'good night' to me properly," the strange lady said.

"What's that?" I said.

"Good night, Mother—that's what you must say to me now," she said.

"No, I won't," I cried, upset.

"Yes, I'm your mother now."

"No, no—aunt!" I screamed.

"Not aunt—you must call me your mother," she said forcefully.

"No, I know who my mother is. You're not my mother. I know where my mother got left. I want to go back, I want to go home," I yelled as loud as I could. "I want to go back to where I came from." I didn't dare to say the name of the place, in case she would be able to find me there again.

"You must forget that now. Forget it—it's a bad dream. It was only a bad dream," she kept saying. "You must forget everything. I'm your mother now."

I jumped up and wanted to get dressed again, get my shoes on, most of all get out of here, get away, get out of this terrible house.

But she wouldn't let me and there was a sort of wrestling match all around my bed, with both of us screaming. I cried and yelled and bit and scratched and kept trying to reach my clothes. But she was stronger and she had longer staying power.

At some point I was exhausted and gave up, and sobbed out some muttered noise that sounded like "mother," and she relented and turned out the light.

I cried for a long time. I thought about my mother's face as she lay there and how she sort of smiled as she gave me the bread.

I felt more ashamed than I had ever felt in my life. I felt as if I'd become a criminal, my mother's betrayer. I felt filthy and wretched, and my skin began to crawl and itch again.

Now I've really turned into a bad person.

Nobody will want me anymore, nobody will like me. What should I do? I would need to ask Motti, or Jankl. They'd know what to do. But they'd maybe chase me away. Nobody wants to be friends with a traitor. I won't ever be able to go back to my people—they'd have so many reasons to take revenge on me. No amount of talking can cover up the terrible thing I just did, there's no way to forgive it.

And here? I can't stay here, it'll just go on like this— I've ended up on the wrong side.

Thinking that, I fell asleep, and dreamed the terrible dream again about the dead world, the black sky, the insects eating me, and the iron cars going up the mountain in their endless chain and disappearing into the yellowish brown jaw under the helmet.

Next day the lady took me through the house and the big garden. She explained to me that I wasn't allowed to tread in the flower beds, and that I could walk on the grass, but not sit—grass stains are very hard to wash out—if I wanted to sit, there was the garden bench.

She showed me the fruit trees, and told me not to get any ideas about pulling fruit down off them. Above all, I was to take care of my new clothes and always take off my shoes after I'd been playing, and wash my hands. She said a lot else, but I don't remember it.

But there was something else—she also showed me the high fence surrounding the garden, and I was told never to climb over it. I looked at her mistrustfully, but nothing moved in her face.

Then we went back into the house and she wanted to show me the cellar.

"This is the laundry room," she said, "and this is the drying room, and that's the food cellar with fruit."

She opened a heavy door, and a dim light was switched on. I could hardly believe my eyes.

There were wooden bunks. And on the wooden bunks were apples, but the bunks looked like the bunks I knew.

I didn't believe anything she said anymore.

Take away the apples and they look just like the stacks of bunks in the barracks! Only smaller, just right for children. I was terrified. What's going on here? Something's not right. Be careful.

She shut the door again.

"And now the coal furnace for the heating. We also heat the water that way," she said without any expression.

She opened another door, this one even heavier. We went around a heap of coal, and there it was.

All I understood about heating until then was that a stove was something in which you burned little bits of wood, and you cooked on it, and warmed your hands.

But this was a huge, black monster, far taller than I was.

The lady opened a semicircular cover, took the shovel, threw some coal inside, and I could see the flames. In deathly fear I stared at the monster.

So—my suspicions were right. I've fallen into a trap. The oven door is smaller than usual, but it's big enough for children. I know, I've seen, they use children for heating too.

Wooden bunks for children, oven doors for children, it's all too much. As I thought this, I suddenly raced up the cellar stairs and into my room. My thoughts were falling over each other. I was right. They're trying to trick me. That's why they want me to forget what I know. The camp's still here. Everything's still here.

They've only got to carry the "fruit racks," the bunks, into the wooden garden house, they've only got to take the cast-iron oven with the children's door and install it out on the stone forecourt outside, the garden's already fenced in, and it would all be just the way it was before, except that this time I'd be alone, totally alone.

The camp's still there, they just hid it. They'll bring it out if I don't obey them.

"Mama, Motti, Jankl, what do I do?" I cried silently into the pillow, but nobody answered.

Years later, the coal system was replaced by a small, modern oil-fired one and I breathed easier: at least this danger seemed to have been banished, but that didn't mean people were to be trusted.

17

"HE HAS TO GO TO SCHOOL as soon as possible," my foster parents said, and that was the beginning of a bad time.

School was full of talk, but nobody had the faintest idea about life—still less about death—not even the teacher. They all behaved as if they were going to live forever.

People talked about things and learned things that simply didn't exist. Mostly, I couldn't understand a thing. I could understand most of the words quite quickly, but when I put them together, they made no sense, no shape that I could project. So I dozed along in class, mostly baffled by what was going on around me.

The strangest problems were explored for hours on end, and the questions asked struck me as completely unreal. Why should I care how many pairs of shoes I can buy with so-and-so much money, if one pair costs such-and-such? Who needs so many shoes? I've only got two feet. And lots of people have no shoes at all, and that's when you get strips of cloth to tie around your feet. Or sometimes you trade your shoes for soup or a mug of water.

"Which stories of Swiss heroes do you all know?" asked the teacher.

Heroes? Did she say heroes?

From somewhere, once, I'd picked up the phrase "heroes of the German Reich," and who they meant were the black uniforms. Are there heroes like that here too? Aren't heroes always the people who kill you?

"Stories of Swiss heroes?" she asks again, and she's pointing at me. I stand up and they're all looking at me. What am I supposed to say? What does she want me to say? I begin to sweat.

"I—I didn't know these heroes were Swiss"—the girls in the benches behind me snicker, and one or two of the boys begin to boo.

The teacher looks at me resignedly, the way she always does when she doesn't understand my answers, and then she unrolls a big colored poster.

"What do you see here?" she asks again.

"Tell! William Tell! The arrow!" they're calling from all the benches.

"So—what do you see? Describe the picture," says the teacher, who's still turned toward me.

I stare in horror at the picture, at this man called Tell, who's obviously a hero, and he's holding a strange weapon and aiming it, and he's aiming it at a child, and the child's just standing there, not knowing what's coming.

I turn away. What has school got to do with me? Why is she showing me this terrible picture? Here in this country, where everyone keeps saying I'm to forget, and that it never happened, I only dreamed it. But they know all about it!

"You're supposed to be looking at the picture—what do you see?" she asks impatiently, and I make myself look at the picture again.

"I see—I see an SS man," I say hesitantly, "and he's shooting at children," I add quickly.

A gale of laughter in the classroom.

"Quiet," barks the teacher, then turns back to me.

"I'm sorry—what did you say?" and I can see that she's getting angry.

"The—the . . ." I'm stuttering now. The girls behind me snicker even louder. They always do that when I stutter.

"The hero's shooting the children, but . . ."

"But what?" the teacher says fiercely. "What do you mean?" Her face is turning red.

". . . But . . . but it's not normal," I say, trying not to cry.

"Who or what isn't normal here?" Now she's beside herself, and shouting. I force down the lump in my throat and try to concentrate. But I can't interpret what's going on. What's this about? Something's coming—what is it? I decide to observe her before I say anything else. I look straight at her face. I see the glittering eyes, the angry, twisted mouth—it's the block warden.

There she stands, legs apart, sturdy, hands on her hips. The teacher's a warden—our block warden. She's just in disguise, she's taken off her uniform. Now she's wearing a red sweater, she's trying to trick me.

"You children are just dirt," she always said. So why is she trying to force me to explain this picture now? She's known all about it forever—she knows what it means.

I try again.

"It's not normal, bec—because . . ." I'm stuttering again.

"Because why?" she says loudly.

"Because our block warden said, 'Bullets are too good for children,' and bec-bec-because only grown-ups get shot . . . or they go into the gas. The children get thrown in the fire, or killed by hand—mostly, that is."

"How do you . . ." she screeches, losing her composure.

"How?—well, using the hands, around the neck, the way they do with hens."

"Sit down and stop talking drivel."

"Drivel?"—another incomprehensible word, but clearly not a good one.

I look over the warden-teacher, standing there shaking with anger, standing there in front of the big blackboard, her hands still on her hips. My eyes begin to smart, and the big blackboard turns watery, gets bigger and bigger until it surrounds the whole classroom and turns into a black sky, and the warden-teacher is standing in front of the black sky in her red pullover, and the red pullover is dripping red blood down in a stream over all the benches. "Red warden—bloody warden," I hear in my head.

She was so feared, the block warden who watched over us back then, and kicked us with her hard boots or "decorated" (as she called it) our stomachs and backs with bloody stripes—the bloody warden, who deliberately poured the little ration of soup so that it missed your bowl and went onto the floor. And took away children, children she swore at and called "dung" or "cameldung" and never brought back again.

"Cameldung"—whatever that was—meant something absolute, something irretrievable, it was the announcement of the end. Lots of us were cameldung.* Now she's found me, too. Now she's ridiculing me, while I have to describe the picture of her hero, the one who shoots children.

I can tell: one day there'll be a banging at the school doors and her hero Tell will come in. He'll say a friendly hello to the warden and she'll say:

"Look, there he is, I found him. That's him! He made the new boy do it, and he's responsible for his death. He's the one who ate the stolen potatoes with Jankl, and managed to get out of the barracks world. I leave the rest to you." And as she's saying it, she points at me.

And Tell will thank her just as politely, then he'll lead me along the long school corridors and down into the courtyard, and take aim at me.

* In Majdanek, inmates in the last stages of starvation were called "camels" because their spines were bowed.

I take another look at the warden-teacher's blood-red sweater, and it slowly turns into a fiery red ball—a huge fire against the black horizon up on the hill, behind the big fence near the big smoking chimney, where the blackboard used to be.

The class has gone wild, they're all yelling. The girls are laughing right out loud now, high mocking laughter, and tapping their foreheads, while the boys point at me and make fists and yell:

"He's raving, there's no such thing. Liar! He's crazy, mad, he's an idiot."

The warden has trouble restoring order. She explains that Tell isn't shooting children, he's shooting the apple on the child's head.

I look at the child. The child's barefoot. No shoes, not even rags on his feet, he's so poor. He hasn't got long to live anyway, I think, without shoes, or rags against the cold and the rats. His feet will freeze to the ground at roll call. And look at his clothes: only a long shirt, tied around the middle, sleeveless, no trousers—he can't survive.

And anyway—SS men don't shoot apples—that's just stupid. It's just another piece of cruelty: the child's hungry, and he's not allowed to eat the apple. A child who's about to die doesn't need an apple. Tell will eat it once he's killed him.

The warden-teacher must know this. She's lying to us, and the other children obviously believe her. How can they? I don't believe one word.

The lesson continues, and I no longer understand what they're saying. The only thing that's clear is that they're all full of awe and admiration when they talk about this hero and SS man Tell, who shoots children.

An SS man doesn't ever aim without firing. I hate the picture. I'll tear it up sometime, secretly.

The warden-teacher didn't hit me as a punishment, she left that to the rest of the class after school. They fell on me in a swarm on the way home—what could I do, against so many? I sat down on the edge of the pavement and let them beat me.

Why do the children ally themselves with her? That's what hurts most, and makes me sad. Why do they do it? Why do they fight me? They're children too. Why doesn't one of them help me?

Then, to save myself, I fly away in my head, and soar through the air, over the houses and roofs, over the evil city and away, following the birds, far away over endless birch forests, lakes, and rivers, I circle pure white clouds and fly on over hills and valleys, I wave at Motti, my eldest brother, who's in a sunny field throwing his hand-made airplane—and it's all beautiful. Motti waves back.

At some point, I realized that the beating had stopped and that the children had gone away. I stood up and went home.

"You're late," my foster mother said angrily, as she looked suspiciously at my dirty clothes. "Why do you always keep getting into fights?"

I shrugged.

"What did you do in school?"

"Nothing special. Just drivel." And I went to my room.

18

I'D ONLY BEEN AT SCHOOL for a few weeks when the teacher said there was going to be an outing. There was a Folk Fair, and we could all go.

"They have a whole town of booths. We'll go there too," she said.

I couldn't imagine what this might be, but I was excited.

"This afternoon we're going to the town," is all I said at home. I didn't want to show my ignorance.

I was excited, but a little frightened too. All sorts of unexpected things could happen, and I would have no grip on them, and they could betray me.

In spite of all the misfortunes I'd had at school, none of the children had got suspicious of me. None of them had hinted that I might belong to the ones with no right to be here, that I belonged to the ones who had no right to share in their comforts.

The fairground was a dazzling sight. I'd never seen so many colors, and everything seemed to be turning or moving in one direction or another.

Children were sitting on brightly painted horses, on fairy-tale animals, others sat in little coaches, in red cars, in little ships—and they all went around in circles, laughing and waving. Lots of them were sitting on little benches that were lifted up high in the air by a huge wheel and then came swaying down again. In amongst all this were colorful market stalls.

"We'll meet at five o'clock at the exit. Don't let anyone be late," called the teacher.

The class split up into individual groups and little clusters and scattered in all directions. The children seemed to know their way around already, and they were holding shiny coins which they showed each other and compared.

I was uncertain. Which way should I go? After a suitable interval, I followed some of the boys, secretly so to speak, in case they noticed that I didn't know how you were supposed to behave here. I wanted to watch what they did and how they did it.

It wasn't easy to follow them through the crowd, but they soon stopped at one of the stands. I hid opposite, behind a black metal bucket on three legs, which was steaming and smelled wonderful. I looked carefully over to the other side—they were still standing there.

"Do you want a hot chestnut?" asked a man's voice.

I just looked at him, and was too shy to ask what a "chestnut" was.

Chewing and smacking his lips, he held out a round hot brown thing to me.

"Thank you," I said and bit into it.

It crunched, and I thought I was chewing wood fibers.

The man roared with laughter and said, "You're so hungry you don't even want to peel it?" and I was ashamed as I spat the shell out onto the ground.

I took another quick peek over at the boys on the other side. They were still there. They were right up at the counter now, and then with a terrible shock I saw that one of them was holding a gun in his hand.

Are there soldier-children here? Have I just found out what they've been hiding from me? was my first thought. The others were talking excitedly to the marksman and pointing at something inside the stall—a painted lady was standing there.

Oh no—is he going to shoot her?—and at that moment I heard the shot. It sounded a bit thin perhaps, but definitely a shot. I looked over, and was relieved—the painted lady was still standing there. So close, and yet he still missed her? Maybe he just wanted to put a scare into her. But I thought it would be advisable to find my own way and stop following the group.

So I wandered around for a long time on my own, marveling at all the activity. It was wonderful how much there was to see and to smell. There were stalls with amazing sweet things, in endless quantities. How did you get some?

I observed the grown-ups and the children. They handed over the coins and got what they wanted, then walked on, chewing.

I didn't have any coins—that was obviously their privilege—but I'd started to feel hungry. People were taking so much away from the stalls. Maybe someone will have something left over, I thought, and remembered the way it had been before:

There were whole days of hunger back then, and I would sit at a street corner, on the steps of an entryway, protected from the rain by the overhang of a balcony, with my hand outstretched and my cap at my feet. I sat that way for hours. Sometimes I got a potato or a piece of turnip, or someone would throw an onion into the hat; sometimes I just got a kick, or someone would spit into my cap.

Suddenly I was hauled roughly up off the ground. A fist pulled at my ear. "What sort of disgusting behavior is this?" someone was barking over my head. "People don't beg! It's forbidden! Have you gone mad? You should be reported to the police!" It was the man from the stall next door.

Laughter and mocking remarks all around me. Some children in my class had found me, they were grinning in a nasty, scornful way. Where am I? was my first thought, then I came to, and realized.

I hastily grabbed the handkerchief that was still lying

in front of me on the ground. I'd spread it out in front of my feet, since I had no cap. None of the children wore caps here.

The handkerchief was empty.

I've no idea how long I'd been sitting on the ground between the stalls, in among all the passing legs.

News of my unheard-of behavior soon spread through the whole school, even my foster parents heard about it, and they were scandalized: I'd disgraced them, there was no need to beg, they gave me plenty to eat, after all, I had everything I needed—what people must think of them now didn't bear thinking about.

Months later, whenever the children in school caught sight of me, they'd begin their chant:

Beggar kid, beggar kid.
There's never enough for the yid.
Beggar kid, beggar kid.

19

I WAS MAYBE TEN YEARS OLD, or twelve, I just don't
know. During school term I lived with my foster parents,
and in the holidays I went back to the Children's Home.
But that winter I was taken to another home on the
Lenzer Heath, and for the first time I saw the Alps in the
snow. It was a beautiful house above the village, near
the edge of the woods. The director of the house and two
women looked after us—we were about fifty children.

I didn't know any of them, and I was alone a lot. The
snow was piled high, and I didn't like walking on the
paths that the director, whom they also called the "ski
instructor," plowed and shoveled clear. What I liked was

wading along beside the paths and the space for traffic in the deep snow, under the weighed-down fir trees. That's what I was used to, and it made me feel safe.

As I was doing my big circle one gray, overcast afternoon, walking along through the silence, a girl suddenly stepped out from behind a tree and stood there a few feet in front of me, without saying a word, staring into my face.

She was from the Children's Home, but I'd only seen her once before, briefly, from behind. She was about my age, thin face. I looked back at her silently. I didn't dare move, just returned her stare, mesmerized. I saw her wide-open eyes, and all of a sudden I knew: these eyes knew it all, they'd seen everything mine had, they knew infinitely more than anyone else in this country. I knew eyes like this, I'd seen them a thousand times, in the camp and later on. They were Mila's eyes. We children used to tell each other everything with these eyes. She knew it, too; she looked straight through my eyes and into my heart.

We were still standing there, motionless.

"I prefer not using the path, just walking in the snow through the wood—it's beautiful," I said.

She nodded.

"It's a little like home," she said softly, and I knew she was thinking of the huge forests we'd left so far behind. Slowly, not talking, but holding hands tightly, we did another big circle around the Children's Home before we went back inside.

The next day the sun came out, the sky was bright, and the snow glittered.

"We can all take a turn on the ski lift today—go and get ready," announced the director–ski instructor. I shrugged—I didn't know what a "ski lift" meant.

They tied wooden boards under my feet—you used them to get through the snow more easily. All the children gathered themselves into a double column outside in front of the house. The girl was suddenly standing in front of me. They'd tied pieces of wood under her feet too. We walked silently in the long line side by side. The director ran up and down the line, supervising.

I kept watch on him. Something about him looked more and more disturbing. Under his long jacket, he was wearing strange battlefield gray trousers, and on his feet were some new kind of heavy shoes. Something was wrong. In anxious silence I hurried along with the girl. The further we went through the wood, and the closer we got to the valley floor, the more loudly we could hear an unfamiliar noise. It was just a humming at first, but then it got louder and louder, ominous and threatening. The thunder of what was clearly a huge engine filled the air until it threatened to suffocate everything in its roar.

I came to a terrified halt in the shelter of the last line of trees, and looked down into the clearing. The girl stopped beside me, shaking, and reached for my hand. The other children pushed past us, laughing. In the clearing was a little house, open on one side. An immense iron wheel was turning inside like some merciless, indifferent mill. The wheel moved two fat steel ropes that ran up the mountainside opposite.

"The death machine," I heard myself saying. My nightmare was coming true.

"Yes," the girl whispered. "This time we've had it."
She was crying without a sound. We stared hypnotized at
the thundering monster.

"The director," I thought suddenly. I had been right to
feel anxious about him. We could see double wooden
hooks hanging down off the steel rope. We watched as
the director and an assistant kept attaching pairs of children to the hooks. A jolt, and the children were carried
off up the mountain by the rope.

My eyes followed the rope, and what I was able to see
through the fir branches was the last proof of the horror
that was under way: there was a house built into the
mountain way up there. But the front of the house was
missing—there was only a huge, yawning black hole that
led right through the house and into the mountain—and
disappearing into it was the steel rope with the children
on the hooks.

The girl followed my look. She leaned against me, and
I could feel her fingers digging into my arm. I turned my
head—she wasn't crying anymore. When I looked at her
eyes, I saw the eyes I remembered very well, of children
who won't come back.

"The grave's inside the mountain," she said slowly, and
I nodded.

"We'll go together?"

I nodded again.

"It's caught up with us," I said.

So the director was also the executioner, and he did his
work fast. The area down there was emptying. We
clutched each other as tightly as we could, and slowly we

reached the death machine, the last ones. A brief feeling of happiness came over me. That must be what people call love, I thought.

We were the only children who knew the truth, and we could rely on each other absolutely, and we were ready to hold hands as we went toward the end.

The executioner positioned us under the steel rope and I saw the double wooden hook coming up on us from behind. The executioner tried to push the hook underneath us. We clung onto each other even tighter. There was a great jerk and we were thrown forward. The hook didn't hold, it seemed to be too big for us. The hook slid upward, banging us on our backs and heads, and disappeared into the air. I thought there must be a chance. The next hook was on its way.

"Lie flat," I whispered.

We fell down in the snow as the hook knocked us from behind again and disappeared. The executioner began to curse furiously in a language I didn't know. We sprawled in the snow half on our knees and half on our stomachs. Squinting sideways, I saw the executioner's heavy shoes next to me.

"Stay down," I whispered again.

The girl reacted quickly, the way we'd learned. She forced her face down in the snow, closed her arms over her head for protection, and tensed her back. I did the same, and we waited for the blows. But nothing happened, except that the death machine sounded even hungrier.

I was afraid that the girl would not be able to hold her head down for long enough. If you brought your head up too soon, there was the danger that you'd get a boot in your face, which could throw you right over so that you landed on your back, leaving your face and stomach unprotected for a moment. But still nothing like that happened.

Suddenly we heard the executioner cursing again. He hauled us up with rough hands and set us ungently on our feet again. We were to return immediately to the Children's Home, he yelled at us with a red face and little yellow eyes. He took the wooden boards off our feet and we ran. We could hear him still calling:

"City kids . . . weaklings . . . scaredy-cats."

We came to a halt under the protective cave of the first trees and looked back, trying to work out what had happened. The clearing down there was empty, with just the roar of the death machine. The girl held tight to my hand and we stared at the double wooden hooks come swinging empty down the mountain.

"You see—nobody's coming back," I whispered, "no one ever comes back."

"They're all dead," said the girl. "We're the only ones who know the secret."

We looked at each other, and we knew we'd never give it away. We walked slowly back through the woods. Suddenly she stopped and I saw that she was crying.

"Aren't you happy?" I asked. "Isn't it better to be alive than dead?"

She looked at me sadly.

"No," she said, "both are terrible. A car is coming to take me away tomorrow. We'll never see each other again."

Sadness poured over me, and I wondered if it had been a good idea to cheat the executioner. It was my fault that instead of dying, we were now going to be alone, each of us, without knowing how we were going to bear it. What had I done?

Next morning I waited under a tree from which I could see the road the car would have to take to get here and go away again with the girl—the road shoveled clear by the executioner.

The car windows were iced over, I couldn't see anything. I don't know if the girl saw me, or if she waved back when I waved to her.

I never once asked her her name.

By noon the sun was shining again and everything was quiet in the home. I saw the executioner—so called "ski instructor"—lying out on his deck chair on the sun terrace. I looked down from the window at him as he slept unawares.

"I have to find a way to kill him."

20

I WAS ALREADY in one of the senior classes at high school, and we had a teacher for both history and German whom I really admired. A tall old man with bushy white hair. He had once been a theater director and producer in Germany, until the Nazis expelled him as an undesirable alien. So he had his own reasons for taking us very thoroughly through twentieth-century history.

When we discussed the Nazi system and the Second World War, I soaked up every word he said, asked endless questions, followed up every suggestion to get hold of additional books, which I then secretly read. My foster parents must not find out. They reacted allergically to all these things, and the entire subject was taboo.

I wanted to know everything. I wanted to absorb every detail and understand every connection. I hoped I would find answers for the pictures that came from my broken childhood memory some nights to stop me going to sleep or to give me terrifying nightmares. I wanted to know what other people had gone through back then. I wanted to compare it with my own earliest memories that I carried around inside me. I wanted to subject them to intelligent reason, and arrange them in a pattern that made sense. But the longer I spent at it, the more I learned and absorbed empirically, the more elusive the answer—in the sense of what actually happened—became. It made me despair.

Why had I, in particular, survived? I hadn't earned that right. I had brought too much guilt on myself for that.

I had handed over the new boy; I was inextricably caught up in the fact of his death. It was only because I was a coward that they killed the new boy. I might perhaps have been able to save him, and I didn't do anything.

I had betrayed my mother and now called a stranger "mother."

I had given up the search for my brothers out of a fear of discovering the truth.

I had deserted the colors, and abandoned my friends in the orphanage in Kraków to their fate. I was sitting here in safe, stuffed Switzerland. I had food, I had clothes, while they were under the stamp of Stalin in Poland, and still belonged among the unwanted.

A bad conscience and the fear of discovery were my

daily companions. History lessons helped me to sort it out, and increased my confusion, all at the same time. In one of our last lessons, the teacher showed us a documentary film about the Nazi period and the camps. Especially the camps. I hardly dared to look. I sat there, numb. I was afraid of giving myself away. Nobody must find out that I came from all that filth and madness. I saw all the human shapes I remembered so well in the streets of the camps, the barracks, the bodies, the starving, the uniforms.

But then came something so unexpected as to be unreal, that I knew nothing about: the narrator made mention, full of pathos, of the liberation of the camps by the Allies. On the screen was the Mauthausen concentration camp near Linz.

The yard of the camp was filled with people, prisoners in their striped clothing. They were laughing and waving. You could see them sitting on all the walls surrounding the yard, in jubilation.

And then, the great moment: through the gates of the camp came an American tank with American soldiers on it, also waving. There seemed to be no words to describe the jubilation. Soldiers went over to the weakened prisoners lying on the ground. They were embraced, comforted, kissed. You could see food being handed out; the sick were tended to and the wounded were being bandaged. And everywhere, over and over again, faces transfixed with happiness at being liberated.

"Liberation—it's not true! That's not how it was! It's a lie—that's not what happened." My hands were tight over my mouth to stop myself screaming at the class. I was shattered. And yet I was looking at what was undeniably documentary footage.

Goddammit—who got freed? And where was I when everyone else was being freed? I was there too, in a camp, and I didn't see anything. No one freed us, and nobody brought us food, and nobody tended us or stroked us the way it happened in the film.

So how was it, back then? We just ran away, without permission. The guards were the first to leave our part of the camp. They fled without a word. And the ones who stayed had no more ammunition to fire at us.

And the people outside the camp, in the countryside and the nearby town—they didn't celebrate when they saw us. They cursed us and said, "Go back to where you came from" and "We thought Hitler had gassed the lot of you—and now you come crawling back again."

These people sided with the uniforms. And they spat at me.

I puzzled furiously over what I could recall—but there was nothing there. No joyous liberation. I never heard the word "liberation" back then, I didn't even know there was such a word.

Nobody ever told me the war was over.

Nobody ever told me that the camp was over, finally, definitely over.

Nobody ever told me that the old times and their evil games and rules were over and I could go forward without fear or threat into a new time and a new world, with new peaceful games and new rules. Not even later.

My foster parents just kept repeating:

"You must forget it all. Forget it, the way you forget a bad dream: you're not to think about it any more. It was all a dream . . ."

It was impossible for me to work out what they really wanted from me. And if I tried to confide in other people, to tell them about it, they would usually listen to the first sentence, then say, "You're making it up!"

How can I forget what I knew? How can I forget what I'm forced to think about every morning when I wake up, and every evening when I go to bed and try to stay awake as long as possible, for fear of the nightmares? How can the scar on my forehead and the knobbly ridge on the back of my head be nothing but the results of a dream?

No, nobody ever said right out to me: Yes, the camp was real, but now it's over. There *is* another world now, and you're allowed to live in it.

So I told myself: All right, you're still stronger than I am. I'll pay constant attention, I'll learn the rules of your games, I'll play your games, but that's all I'll do—play them—I'll never become like you. You people, you profess to take these rules seriously. You preach honesty, and you're liars. You preach openness, and you won't tell me the truth.

Making me play along, making me adopt your rules, is just one of your tricks to soften me up and lull me into a false sense of security. There are the real rules, about living and surviving, that I learned in the camp, and that Jankl taught me, and you'll never get me to forget those.

The good life is nothing but a trap. The camp's still there—just hidden and well disguised. They've taken off their uniforms and dressed themselves up in nice clothes so as not to be recognized.

But listen carefully and watch how they disregard their own nice rules of the game. Just give them the gentlest of hints that maybe, possibly, you're a Jew—and you'll feel it: these are still the same people, and I'm sure of it. They can still kill, even out of uniform.

I had had lots of this kind of long conversation with myself when I was a boy. And now I saw this incontrovertible documentary about the liberation of Mauthausen and other camps.

I went home as if anesthetized, threw down my schoolbag, and went out into the garden. As I often did when I wanted to be left alone to think through something, I climbed high up into one of the beautiful old fir trees and settled myself comfortably on a perch I'd knocked together up there.

From here I could look out over most of the town. The gentle swaying of the treetop was soothing. I was safe up there. Nobody could follow me; I could think.

I replayed the laughing faces of the freed prisoners, their look of relief on the film. Given that the film wasn't lying, given that these faces weren't lying, where was I? What did they conceal from me? Why wasn't I there, too? Did something really happen there and I knew nothing about it?

I became more and more unsure, and a terrible suspicion began to eat its way into me like a gnawing pain. It clawed into my stomach, lay heavily on my chest, and rose chokingly into my throat:

Perhaps it's true—somehow I missed my own liberation.

I often used to go back and visit my first great physics teacher, Salvo Berkovici, although I'd been studying in another city for a long time by then.

He was an old man, and a wise one. The last surviving member of a centuries-old family of Romanian rabbis, he had studied, among other things, music, physics, mathematics, philosophy, and medicine. He was my guide and mentor, the kind of father I would have wished for myself.

He was the only person with whom I could be open. He was the only person back then who understood if all I could dare do was to hint at past events.

He understood what I was really saying.

AFTERWORD

I GREW UP and became an adult in a time and in a society that didn't want to listen, or perhaps was incapable of listening. "Children have no memories, children forget quickly, you must forget it all, it was just a bad dream." These were the words, endlessly repeated, that were used on me from my schooldays to erase my past and make me keep quiet. So for decades I was silent, but my memory could not be wiped clean. Very occasionally I would make timid attempts to share at least some parts of it with someone, but these attempts always went wrong. A finger tapping against the forehead or aggressive questions in return soon made me fall silent, taking back what I'd revealed. It is so easy to make a child mistrust his own reflections, to take away his voice. I wanted my own certainty back, and I wanted my voice back, so I began to write.

It is only in recent years that the Children of the Holocaust societies came into existence in Warsaw and the United States, that the AMCHA organization was formed in Israel, and that historians and psychologists began to tackle the questions and the problems of children who survived the Shoa. I am in contact with many of them—historians, psychologists, and victims—and I have worked with some of them for years. Several hundred children who survived the Shoah have come forward. They are "children without identity," lacking any certain information about their origins, with all traces carefully erased, furnished with false names and often with false papers too. They grew up with a pseudo-identity which in Eastern Europe protected them from discrimination, and in Western Europe, from being sent back east as stateless persons.

As a child, I also received a new identity, another name, another date and place of birth. The document I hold in my hands—a makeshift summary, no actual birth certificate—gives the date of my birth as February 12, 1941. But this date has nothing to do with either the history of this century or my personal history. I have now taken legal steps to have this imposed identity annulled.

Legally accredited truth is one thing—the truth of a life another. Years of research, many journeys back to the places where I remember things happened, and countless conversations with specialists and historians have helped me to clarify many previously inexplicable shreds of memory, to identify places and people, to find them again and to make a possible, more or less logical chronology out of it. I thank them all.

I wrote these fragments of memory to explore both myself and my earliest childhood; it may also have been an attempt to set myself free. And I wrote them with the hope that perhaps other people in the same situation would find the necessary support and strength to cry out their own traumatic childhood memories, so that they too could learn that there really are people today who will take them seriously, and who want to listen and to understand.

They should know that they are not alone.

JUNE 1995